DUSKY MAIDENS

DUSKY MAIDENS

THE ODYSSEY OF THE EARLY BLACK DRAMATIC ACTRESS

Jo A. Tanner

Contributions in
Afro-American and African Studies,
Number 156

GREENWOOD PRESS
WESTPORT, CONNECTICUT • LONDON

Library of Congress Cataloging-in-Publication Data

Tanner, Jo A.
  Dusky maidens / the odyssey of the early black dramatic actress /
Jo A. Tanner.
      p.   cm. – (Contributions in Afro-American and African
Studies, ISSN 0069-9624 ; no. 156)
    ISBN 0-313-27717-6
    1. Afro-American actresses – Biography.   2. Theater – United States –
History.   3. Women in the theater – United States.   I. Title.
II. Series.
PN2286.T36   1993
792'.028'092273 – dc20   92-18349

British Library Cataloguing in Publication Data is available.

Library of Congress Catalog Card Number: 92-18349
ISBN: 0-313-27717-6
ISSN: 0069-9624

First published in 1992

Greenwood Press, 88 Post Road West, Westport, CT 06881
An imprint of Greenwood Publishing Group, Inc.

Printed in the United States of America

The paper used in this book complies with the
Permanent Paper Standard issued by the National
Information Standards Organization (Z39.48-1984).

10 9 8 7 6 5 4 3 2

Copyright Acknowledgments

Every reasonable effort has been made to trace the owners of copyright materials in this
book, but in some instances this has proven impossible. The author and publisher will be
glad to receive information leading to more complete acknowledgments in subsequent
printings of the book and in the meantime extend their apologies for any omissions.

For the women in my family

CONTENTS

PHOTOGRAPHS

PREFACE

My interest in early American theatre history was sparked while taking a course in the history and criticism of nineteenth-century American drama and theatre. During the class, I was introduced to an actress/playwright named Anna Cora Mowatt (1819–1870). The daughter of a wealthy New York merchant and the granddaughter of a signer of the Declaration of Independence, Mowatt in 1845 wrote *Fashion*, the first successful American comedy. A few months later she debuted at the Park Theatre in New York as Pauline in *The Lady of Lyons*. An immediate success, she toured throughout America and England. Remembered more for her acting than for her writing, Mowatt received star billing wherever she appeared.[1]

Unlike most women, Anna Cora Mowatt began her acting career at the top. From my discovery of how she became an actress evolved questions concerning the Black dramatic actress: Who was the first Black woman to perform in drama on the American stage? What were the dominant influences on her emergence and development? As a Black female performer and theatre student, I was attempting to make early American theatre history relevant to me. Needless to say, there was not a single reference made regarding Black women throughout the entire term. Frustrated, I set out to uncover the legacy of the Black dramatic actress.

I learned that prior to 1917, Black performers had little opportunity professionally to act in serious plays. Moreover, due to the impact of racial and sexual oppression, the evolution of the Black dramatic actress had been severely hindered. Though Black women had been performing on the professional concert stage since the early 1850s and on the professional theatrical stage since the 1860s, it was not until the 1890s, in Black musical shows, that they gained real prominence on the American stage. Later, some made a transition from musicals to straight dramatic plays.

A direct, almost evolutionary, line can be traced from the Black musicals of the 1890s to Ridgely Torrence's *Three Plays for a Negro Theatre* (1917), the first *dramatic* presentation on the Broadway stage in which Black actresses appeared. A number of these women began their careers in Black musical shows at the turn of the century, careers that would last over forty years. Transcending double discrimination, these turn-of-the-century actresses made the successful transition from musicals to drama, and refuted the generally held belief that while Black performers were natural singers and dancers, they did not possess the ability to portray dramatic characters. In so doing, they began the odyssey of the evolving pattern of many Black actresses.

The lives of several Black actresses, who appeared on the mainstream professional stage and on the professional Black stage (e.g., the Lafayette Theatre) in New York, as well as nationally and internationally, illustrate this evolutionary cycle. Their careers span from the turn of the century when African Americans were performing in blackface to a generation that faced the social awareness engendered by World War II. What was the impact of these entertainers on the image and development of the Black performer, on the development of Black musical comedy and legitimate drama, and on the evolution of mainstream American theatre itself?

Theatrical history books, biographical references, and journals of the period, if they do not omit Black women, merely mention them. Biographical dictionaries of Blacks and histories and bibliographies of Blacks in American theatre do include some references to women, but to date there has been no study that has focused primarily on the attributes and achievements of early Black female performers.

This is the story of the evolution of the Black dramatic actress. It is a largely untold story that fills a gap in the annals of American theatrical history. Further, it permanently records in one location the often unheralded accomplishments of those trailblazers who helped to pave the way for contemporary Black actresses. By placing these turn-of-the-century entertainers in a historical context, we can better understand the magnitude of their contributions.

Research for the book includes articles, reviews, plays, playbills, personal scrapbooks, dissertations, books, bibliographies, and taped interviews. Not all of the biographical data on Black women performers of this period (i.e., dates and places of birth, marriage, death, and education) can be established from available materials. Some details of roles, places, and dates of performances cannot be found. We can, however, using bits and pieces from numerous sources, patch together the lives and careers of these entertainers. They were among the most talented women in the country and perhaps the world. These actresses, singers, and dancers achieved recognition in their own right, and are representative of those performers whose careers are most fully documented. Their activities are typical of what some of their contemporaries were trying to do and to some extent accomplished.

These pioneers were admired, especially in Europe, but were never fully accepted at home. Nonetheless, through their efforts we can trace the beginnings of the reentry (with minstrelsy being the first entry) of Blacks on the professional stage in musical shows, and later in legitimate drama. It was this gradual change from musicals to drama that made possible the comparatively recent acclaim for serious acting talent evidenced by the careers of such Black actresses as Diana Sands, Ruby Dee, Frances Foster, Rosaline Cash, Abbey Lincoln, Diahann Carroll, Clarice Taylor, Cicely Tyson, Mary Alice, Gloria Foster, Helen Martin, Rosetta LeNoire, and Esther Rolle.[2]

Acknowledgments

I am grateful to my distinguished mentors, Stanley A. Waren, Vera M. Roberts, and James V. Hatch, for their scholarship and dedication, as well as their personal support. I am also indebted to James Hatch for making his extensive Black Theatre collection, the Hatch-Billops Collection, available to me. I would like to thank Margaret Knapp for her assistance during the early stages of the project. I would like to extend my appreciation to Helen Armstead-Johnson. Her work on early Black performers, especially women, inspired me to continue researching and writing on the subject.

An acknowledgment must go to Queens College/CUNY and the Drama, Theatre, and Dance department for their contributions. I am particularly grateful to my friend and colleague Edward M. Greenberg for providing valuable suggestions during our numerous conversations.

My gratitude also goes to those at Greenwood Press who have been directly involved with the publication of this book. A special thanks to Marilyn Brownstein for her enthusiastic response to my work.

My warmest thanks go to my best friend Dean K. Harrison. His continued support and encouragement over the years will never be forgotten.

Dusky Maidens

Introduction: A Historical Overview

THE BLACK WOMAN IN AMERICA, 1890–1917

"The black woman is the forgotten heroine of our history," declared feminist historian Gerda Lerner. She continued, "Sentimentalized and stereotyped as the 'Mammy' of fiction, the black woman has never yet received her due. Her accomplishment in bearing her hard lot without rancor and caring for the master's offspring with warmth and affection, and in providing her own family with whatever stability was possible was truly remarkable."[1]

Like White women, Black women were denied the ballot until 1920. One of the conspicuous facts concerning the history of Black women is that they have been faced with double discrimination. In addition to sharing all the restrictions of sex oppression with White women, they have been further handicapped by the restrictions of race oppression shared by Black Americans.

After the failure of Reconstruction governments and the Compromise of 1877, reconciliation between the states, not social injustice, was the main political issue. With the rise of nationalism came increased anti-Black prejudice, particularly in the South. In 1890 Mississippi became the first state to include disfranchisement laws in its constitution. During the 1880s and 1890s other Southern states adopted segregated school and railroad systems. Lynchings, mostly in the South, peaked during the 1880s and early 1890s, averaging 150 yearly and reaching 235 in 1892.[2]

Even though Blacks in the North retained their civil and political rights legally, their position was only little better than Blacks in the South. In 1883, after the Supreme Court declared the Civil Rights Act of 1875 unconstitutional, most Northern states enacted legislation supporting the Fourteenth Amendment, which prohibited discrimination in public places.[3] "Such laws, however, were often of little value in the face of hostile public opinion," explained August Meier. "Relatively few cases came before the courts, and local customs, particularly in areas contiguous to the South, often acted as an effective deterrent to the exercise of the rights guaranteed by legislation."[4]

By 1880 Northern Blacks had established their rights to an education, and by 1900 had achieved legal integration in public schools. Black teachers, however, often were not permitted to work in "the mixed school system." Moreover, along the Mason-Dixon line and in the Ohio Valley, education laws were usually ignored. The economic picture for Blacks in the nation was bleak. In the North they were limited to unskilled labor and menial jobs while most Blacks in the South continued to barely earn a living as laborers and sharecroppers. Both Northern and Southern unions and urban employers practiced discrimination. Unions became segregated during the 1890s, causing Black workers in skilled trades to decline in the South. Also, Northern Blacks were being replaced by immigrants in domestic service.[5]

As Whites grew more hostile, Blacks reacted by adopting racial solidarity, self-help doctrines, and better economic development as more effective ways of obtaining racial advancement than integration and politics.[6] Nonetheless, because of the economic, social, and cultural issues, questions, and dilemmas concerning Blacks at the time, they were faced with the problem of defining and clarifying their status. Due to their cultural history in American society, however, Blacks experienced what Black scholar and founding editor of *The Crisis* W.E.B. Du Bois referred to in *The Souls of Black Folk* (1903) as "double consciousness."

> The Negro is a sort of seventh son, born with a veil, and gifted with second-sight in this American nation, – a world which yields him no true self-consciousness, but only lets him see himself through the revelation of the other world. It is a peculiar sensation, this double-consciousness, this sense of always looking at one's self through the eyes of others, of measuring one's soul by the tape of a world that looks on in amused contempt and pity. One ever feels his twoness, – an American, a Negro; two warring souls, two thoughts, two unreciled strivings; two warring ideals in one dark body, whose dogged strength alone keeps it from being torn asunder.[7]

From 1865 to 1917, nearly 90 percent of all Black Americans lived in the South. They made up 30 percent of the total Southern population; more than half of them lived in counties that were 50 percent or more Black. As late as 1900, the life expectancy of Black women was only 33.5 years. LaFrances Rodgers-Rose, editor of *The Black Woman*, correlated the early deaths of Black women to the high mortality rate among Black infants.[8] Yet the first generation of Black women after slavery were making progress in controlling their lives. They were marrying later and having fewer children, noted Paula Giddings.[9]

At the turn of the century, most Black women were married and living with their husbands. Even though racial oppression deeply affected family life, establishing patterns different from the prevailing male-dominated family of White Americans, families headed by Black women from slavery to 1960 never exceeded 25 percent. More female-headed households existed in urban areas than in rural areas.[10]

The extended family structure did develop, however. According to sociologist Andrew Billingsley, "extended families include other relatives or in-laws of the family head, sharing the same household with the nuclear family."[11] Despite its negative origins, there was an advantage to the development of this type of family pattern. "This family structure, in which all children, regardless of the marital or economic status of their families, are ensured a modicum of security, represents a useful adaptation for group survival by an economically depressed community," noted Lerner.[12]

Due to racial discrimination, most Black men have been economically oppressed. Consequently, in contrast to White women who entered the job market in large numbers only in the twentieth century, many Black women had to work to take care of themselves and their families. Because of race and sex restrictions, the job opportunities available to Black women were limited. The first Black female lawyer graduated in 1887 and some Black women physicians were practicing as early as the 1860s.[13] At the end of the first decade of the twentieth century, however, there were only two Black women attorneys compared to 796 Black male attorneys. Out of 3,007 Black doctors, only 333 were women. Of all Black female workers, only 1 percent, or 22,450, were teachers. There were 135 Black bankers, but only thirteen were women. For the most part, Black women earned their living working either in agriculture, as servants, or as laundresses.[14]

From 1890 to 1910, nearly 200,000 Blacks left the farms and migrated to the cities, both Northern and Southern.[15] Most were employed as servants, janitors, waiters, and laundresses. By 1890, 70 percent of all Black men in New York City were either personal or domestic servants, compared to 25 percent of foreign-born men and 20 percent of the city's total male population. On the other hand, Black women were employed as domestics to a greater degree than all other New Yorkers. In addition, when they entered the industrial field, Black women were placed in the least desirable positions at the poorest pay. By 1910, only 4.2 percent of the city's married White women worked compared to 31.4 percent of the city's married Black women. From 1890 to 1920, a higher rate of widowhood among New York's Black women than among foreign and native-born women was one of the factors that forced them to seek employment.[16]

Lerner observed that "the only hope for a [Black] girl to escape the unskilled, service job trap was in getting a professional education."[17] During this time, one of the few educational opportunities open to Black women was teaching. Black women attended both Black and White colleges including Wellesley, Radcliffe, Cornell, and Oberlin, among others both here and abroad. In an attempt to overcome some of the political, social, and economic problems facing Black women enrolled in college, the two largest Black women's sororities were founded: Alpha Kappa Alpha and Delta Sigma Theta in 1911 and 1913, respectively.[18]

After graduating, many of these women went on to help educate their people. Among them was Lucy Laney, who in 1886 started the Haines Normal Institute in Atlanta, Georgia. In 1902 Charlotte Hawkins Brown founded a school for Black girls, the Palmer Memorial Institute in Sedalia, North Carolina. In 1904 Mary McLeod Bethune began a school on a garbage dump in Daytona Beach, Florida. Today it is the well-known Bethune-Cookman College.[19] Both Brown and Bethune were protégées of Lucy Laney.[20] "Although growing numbers of Black women had the opportunity to enter college and the professions, the masses of Black women were still relegated to domestic and menial work," wrote Giddings. "They were excluded from such job categories as clerk and secretary, newly opened to women (who were being hired to replace men at lower wages), because White women wanted them."[21]

The sexual exploitation of Black women by White men is a key feature of racial oppression in America that has continued from slavery until the late 1960s when it was checked by the rise of the militancy of the Black nationalist movement.[22] In an attempt to justify the myth that Black women were totally responsible for their own victimization, regardless of class, they were stereotyped as being immoral.[23] Summing up the dominant attitudes toward Black women, Giddings quoted material published in *The Independent,* a contemporary newspaper. " 'Like White women,' one writer said, 'Black women had the brains of a child, the passion of a woman,' but unlike Whites, Black women were 'steeped in centuries of ignorance and savagery, and wrapped about with immoral vices.' "[24]

This was the time for Black women to defend their moral integrity. One of the first public opportunities to do so came during the World Columbian Exposition of 1893. Haiti participated in the exhibit featuring women's accomplishments. Black women as a group were excluded, however, because they were not part of a "national women's organization."[25] However, a few Black women, the "exceptions," speakers who were considered "safe" by the Lady Managers, were invited. Among them, Fannie Barrier Williams, who was born of middle-class parents, was graduated from the New England Conservatory of Music, and was one of the few Black members of the Chicago Women's Club, did not sidestep the issue.[26] She told her audience, " 'I regret the necessity of speaking of the moral question of our women, . . . the morality of our home life has been commented on so disparagingly and meanly that we are placed in the unfortunate position of being defenders of our name.' "[27]

Anna Julia Cooper, a Black writer and educator, also attended the event. "What White feminists hardly realized," noted Giddings, "was that Black women were providing them a means for their own liberation. For inherent in the Black women's defense of their integrity was a challenge to the Victorian ideas that kept all women oppressed."[28]

As indicated above, during the 1890s one of the problems of racism was the lynching of Black men who were usually charged with raping White women. Ida B. Wells, an educator and Black spokesperson for women's rights and civil rights, linked the sexual oppression of Black women with the lynching (racial oppression) of Black men, which reinforced the double sex standards. A most outspoken fighter against lynching, Wells had always been a person who demanded justice. In 1884 Wells was dragged from her seat in the "Ladies' Coach" on a train to Memphis because she refused to sit in the smoking car. She sued the Chesapeake and Ohio Railroad and won.[29] "Wells was the first Afro-American to challenge the 1883 nullification of the Civil Rights Bill passed during Reconstruction," wrote Giddings. "Her victory would have set a significant precedent – a fact not lost on the Tennessee Supreme Court, which reversed the lower court's decision."[30]

During the 1880s, there were nearly 200 Black newspapers and Wells's articles "about everything from compelling national issues to local community ones,"[31] appeared in the best papers. In 1891, after she was fired from her teaching job for writing an article in the Memphis *Free Press* exposing discrimination in the Memphis school system, Wells (whose pen name was "Iola") began writing full time. As she was investigating 728 cases of lynching that had taken place during the last ten years, two more occurred. Angered, Wells took to the press and told her readers, " 'Nobody in this section of the country believed the threadbare lie that Negro men rape white women. If Southern white

men are not careful, they will overreach themselves and public senti-
ment will have a reaction. A conclusion will then be reached which will
be very damaging to the moral reputation of their women.' "[32]

Wells, who was in New York when the editorial appeared, was
banned from returning to the South. She purchased a gun and began
raising money to publish her findings in a booklet entitled "Southern
Horror: Lynch Law in All Its Phases." On 5 June 1892, the *New York
Age,* a Harlem weekly, printed her article on lynching. The study,
which included cases involving women and children, reported "names,
dates, places and circumstances of hundreds of lynchings for alleged
rape. The response to the article was sensational and Fortune [the edi-
tor] published ten thousand copies of the issue."[33] A good businesswoman, Wells used her 3,000-name subscription list from the *Free
Press,* of which she was part owner, to buy one-fourth of the *New York
Age.*[34]

Wells toured the Northern states and the British Isles speaking
against lynching and for women's rights, gaining international attention. After returning from England, Wells attended the Columbian Exposition where she, Frederick Douglass, and her husband-to-be,
Ferdinand Barnett, a lawyer and publisher of *The Conservator,* Chicago's first Black newspaper, distributed their pamphlet on "The Reason
Why The Colored American Is Not in the Columbian Exposition."[35]

On Wells's second trip to England, after the Exposition, she accused
liberal White Americans of condoning lynching. Frances Willard, the
liberal president of the Women's Christian Temperance Union, was also
in England at the time. Angered by Wells's comments, Willard and
Lady Somerset, her English counterpart, tried to keep Wells from the
press. In America, Wells received bad press.[36] *"The New York Times*
ran an article insisting that Black men were prone to rape, and that
Wells, was a 'slanderous and nasty-minded mulatress,' who was looking
for more 'income' than 'outcome.' "[37] The negative response of the
American press to Wells's charges served to rally the English to her
cause. As one British editor wrote, " 'It is idle for men to say that the
conditions which Miss Wells describes do not exist.' "[38]

This trip to England, which was a personal triumph for Wells, had an
impact on the anti-lynching campaign. Several of the British elite
joined the British Anti-Lynching Committee, making their influence
available to her here and abroad. Through the efforts of Wells, lynchings declined in 1893 and continued to do so.[39] Inspired by Wells's determination and success, other Black women began to organize on
behalf of Blacks and women.

In 1895 Josephine St. Piere Ruffin, wife of the first Black judge in

Massachusetts and a Black member of the New England Women's Club, called for a national convention of Black women in Boston.[40] In July over 100 women from ten states attended, forming the National Federation of Afro-American Women. Margaret Murray Washington, Booker T. Washington's third wife, was elected president. Meanwhile, Mary Church Terrell, the daughter of one of the first Black millionaires, had founded the League of Colored Women in Washington, D.C. In 1896 the two groups joined, forming the National Association of Colored Women (NACW), the first national Black organization, predating the NAACP (1909) and the National Urban League (1911). By 1916 the club represented over 50,000 women in more than 1,000 clubs.[41]

Both the NACW and its White counterpart, the General Federation of Women's Clubs, were concerned with social reform and women's rights. The Black women, however, understood that the gaining of their rights was tied to advancing the civil rights of all Black Americans. These women accepted the responsibility of uplifting their people. Their aim, said Terrell, was to " 'build the foundation of the next generation upon such a rock of morality, intelligence and strength, that the floods of proscription, prejudice and persecution may descend upon it in torrents and yet it will not be moved.' "[42]

The NACW achieved a number of accomplishments in a short time. By 1916 they had provided scholarship loans for women to attend college; aided employment and training for both urban and rural Blacks; and founded health care centers and child care programs. The breakthroughs of the NACW were also reflected in the social and artistic achievements of Black women at large. They were being recognized in literature: Emma Dunham Kelly's novel *Megda* (1891), Frances Ellen Harper's *Iola Leroy* (1892), and Pauline Hopkins's *Contending Forces* (1900). Alice Dunbar Nelson published two volumes of poetry, *Violets and Other Tales* (1894) and *The Goodness of St. Tocque* (1899). Marie Selika and Flora Batson were breaking into the classical music field.[43] As Giddings pointed out,

> It may have been no coincidence that during the same year that Black women began demanding to be recognized as "an integral part of the general womanhood of American civilization" . . . they also began to express the full range of their artistic talents. As the club movement shattered the stereotypes of Black women, so did the women emerge in a new light. By the turn of the century, *The Creole Show* became the first theatrical production to break with the minstrel tradition and the first production to feature attractively costumed, "glamorous" Black women.[44]

This landmark production paved the way for Black female stars such as Sissieretta Jones, Dora Dean, Ida Forsyne, Laura Bowman, Anita Bush, and Abbie Mitchell. Because of such developments, they gained prominence and respect on the American stage. As Ada Overton Walker (wife of the famous comic George Walker and a star in her own right) put it, "the Black woman 'no longer lost her dignity when she entered the theater.' "[45]

THE BLACK THEATRE

Show business provided a major opportunity for Blacks to merge into mainstream American society. However, the Black performer and American show business have endured a symbiotic but bittersweet relationship. Despite their many contributions in music, dance, and drama, Black entertainers have generally been restricted to performing within a prescribed framework that permits only limited opportunity and acceptance.

Participation in American theatre by Black women has been severely restricted. Blacks have "been depicted most often as negative stereotypes: the contented slave, the wretched freeman, the comic Negro, and the exotic primitive," according to Jeanne-Marie Miller.[46] She continued: "Black female characters have been scarce in only one of these categories – the brute Negro. They have been more plentiful as the faithful servant. In American drama, where seemingly many more roles have been written for men than women, Black or white, it is the Black female who has faced double discrimination – that of sex and race."[47]

The first Black female character appeared on the American stage as a comic servant in William Milns's *All in a Bustle; or, The New House* on 29 January 1798 at the Park Theatre in New York.[48] This farce "describes the difficulties under which John Hodgkins labored as stage manager of the new theatre. The jealousy of the actresses as to their dressing rooms is well portrayed, and there is a 'black wench' who, in the intervals of waiting on them, falls on the scenery and wipes it up with her head."[49]

A White actress played the part; at the time, Black women were not allowed to perform on the professional stage. In 1823 a Black woman did "perform," as a comic servant, on the American stage. Edwin Forrest was preparing to play the role of Rubin, a Black, in a farce, *The Tailor in Distress,* at the Globe Theatre in Cincinnati. Unable to find a White actress willing to blacken her face, he hired an old Black washerwoman to assist him. It is reported that they were hilarious, and Forrest was a success.[50]

During this period in New York, Blacks, who were not welcome in the legitimate theatre as either audience or artists, attempted to establish their own theatre. In August 1821, the African Grove, a garden where Blacks could enjoy light refreshments, opened at the corner of Bleecker and Mercer Streets. In September the African Theatre (the upper apartment of the African Grove) opened in conjunction with the tea garden.[51] Between 1821 and 1823 Mr. Brown, a West Indian, managed the African Theatre. This semiprofessional stock acting group performed *Richard III, Othello,* and *Tom and Jerry; or, Life in London,* as well as "opera," pantomime, and original material.[52]

The first presentation given by the African company was an adaptation of *Richard III* with an all-male cast. Because the White press found these actors and their efforts a subject for ridicule, the reviews may not give an accurate impression of their performances. Nonetheless, the 21 September 1821 edition of the *Nation Advocate* satirically reported:

> a little dapper, woolly-headed waiter at the City Hotel personated the royal Plantagenet. As may be supposed, some difficulties occurred in the cast of characters and suitable costumes. Richard III had some robes made up from discarded merino curtains of the ball-rooms; and from a paucity of actors, some doublets occurred, as these: King Henry and the Duchess Dowager were represented by one and the same person, while Lady Ann and Catesby were sustained by another. The room was decorated with some taste, and chairs were placed by the wings for clarinets.
>
> The person of Richard was on the whole not amiss; it was perceived that the actor had made the King hump-back instead of crooked back, having literally a hump behind his neck little less than a camel's. Shaping "the legs of unequal size" was also difficult, but was overcome by placing false calves before, and wearing a high-heeled shoe. The entrance of Richard was greeted with loud applause and shaking of handkerchiefs by the black ladies in the front seats and many whispers went around of "How well he looks." . . . Several fashionable songs, sung with no mean taste, concluded the evenings amusement, and the sable audience retired peaceable to their homes. Richard and Catesby were unfortunately taken up by the watch [i.e., they were arrested].[53]

A few weeks later, the company had expanded and added women. George C. D. Odell's *Annals of the New York Stage* included a playbill, dated 1 October 1821, announcing a benefit for the company's leading actor, James Hewlett. The evening's offering featured *Richard III,* with a Miss Welsh playing both the Prince of Wales and Lady Ann and a

Miss J. Welsh as Elizabeth. There was also a pantomime, *Asama* by Hewlett, in which Miss S. Welsh played Asana and Hewlett played Asama, and a ballet, with Miss S. Welch as Columbine.[54]

Langston Hughes and Milton Meltzer have an undated playbill for the African Company in their book *Black Magic.* The evening's bill presented *Tom and Jerry; or, Life in London,* with a Miss Peterson playing Miss Tartan; a Miss Johnson was Jane and later on, in the last scene, she doubled as Mr. Davis; a Miss Davis also played a male part, Cate; and a Miss Foot was Sue. The program also included *On the Slave Market,* Songs and Dances, and ended with the pantomime of *Obi; or, Three Finger'd Jack.* The house seated 300 to 400 patrons, and the prices for this performance were 75¢, 50¢, and 37½¢ for the box, pit, and gallery, respectively.[55] As the popularity of the African Theatre grew, Whites began to attend. In order to "accommodate" them, the 27 October 1821 edition of the *National Advocate* reported that "they have graciously made a partition at the back of their house for the accommodation of the whites."[56]

In January 1822 the African Company moved to the hotel next door to the Park Theatre, challenging the White theatre establishment. This intrusion did not go unnoticed by Whites. They reacted immediately, showing this troupe that they were not welcome. The 10 January 1822 edition of the *American* reported that "the audiences were generally of a riotous character, and amused themselves by throwing crackers on the stage, and cracking their jokes with the actors, until danger from fire and civil discord rendered it necessary to break up the establishment."[57] Defying the police, they continued to act nightly. During a performance of *Richard III,* however, they were arrested and jailed. The group was released only after "they plead [sic] so hard in black verse, and promised [sic] never to act Shakespeare again that the Police Magistrates released them at a very late hour."[58]

Another account of this incident is described in *Memoir and Theatrical Career of Ira Aldridge, the African Roscius,* published in 1849:

> One Stephen Price, a manager of some repute, became actually jealous of the success of the "real Ethiopians" and emissaries were employed to put them down. They attracted considerable notice; and people who went to ridicule remained to admire, albeit there must have been ample scope for the suggestion of the ridiculous. Riots ensued, and destruction fell upon the little theatre. Of course, there was no protection or redress to be obtained from the magistracy (for, unhappily, they were whites), and the company dissolved, much to the chagrin of the Juliet elect, who declared that nothing but envy prevented the blacks from putting the whites completely out of countenance.[59]

The African Company did not dissolve, moving back to the theatre on Bleecker and Mercer streets where they continued to perform. A last public notice of the troupe announced a benefit for Brown, the manager, on 20 and 21 June 1823. For this program they presented *King Shotaway*. Written by Brown and featuring Hewlett as Shotaway, the play is significant as the first American *drama* by a Black playwright.[60] *King Shotaway* chronicled some of Brown's experiences with the insurrection of the Caravs against the British on the Island of St. Vincent.[61] Odell acknowledged the event, saying "First Negro drama, Hail!"[62] The African Theatre was forced to close due to rowdy White spectators, but James Hewlett continued to entertain until 1831. On 22 September, Mrs. Hewlett accompanied her husband on piano, at his retirement benefit at Columbian Hall.[63]

Despite its brief and turbulent existence, the great Black tragedian Ira Aldridge "made his acting debut at the theatre on Mercer street in 1820 or 1821 as Rolla in *Pizarro*. He also performed Romeo, and his work in the African Theatre helped him decide to become an actor."[64] From the 1849 *Memoir*, we learn that the actress who played Cora opposite Aldridge's Rolla " 'was *very* black, requiring no small quantity of whiting, yellow ochre, and vermilion to bring her cheeks to the hue of roses and lilies,' such a face as Sheridan describes in the text."[65] Unfortunately, the names of the actresses who played Cora and Juliet were not mentioned. As with the identities of other Black women in American theatre, they are lost to history.

During the same time of the suppression of the African Theatre, a new image of Black Americans began to appear on the stage, an image that would dominate until the turn of the century. Herbert Marshall and Mildred Stock observed a connection between the two occurrences:

> Growing reaction throughout the country and the hardening of white prejudice against blacks carried with it the demise of the Negro theatre, but curiously, it was at the very time (1823) that the white actor, Edwin Forrest, "represented on the stage the Southern plantation Negro with all his peculiarities of dress, gait, accent, dialect, and manners." So the genuine Negro performers in America were forced out to make way for the white "nigger minstrels." . . .[66]

Blacks entering show business after slavery had two objectives: "first, to make money to help educate our younger ones," pointed out pioneer entertainer Tom Fletcher, "and second, to try to break down the ill feeling that existed toward the colored people."[67] Early Black performers knew that they would be confronted with contempt and scorn. Nevertheless, they eagerly accepted the challenge of embarking on an uncharted yet promising path. By so doing, they began the odyssey that led to the development of the Black theatre.

The Black performer made his debut on the professional legitimate stage in the late 1860s in minstrelsy,[68] the most popular form of entertainment during the mid-nineteenth century. According to cultural historian Margaret Just Butcher,

> Because the comic side of the Negro offered no offense or challenge to the South's tradition of the Negro's subordinate status, it richly colored Southern local and regional culture, and eventually that of the whole nation. The impoverished plantation entertainment of ragamuffin groups of dancing, singing, jigging, and grinning slaves, was the genesis of a major form of the American theater: blackface minstrelsy and its later stepchild, vaudeville. Together they dominated the national stage for a period of at least seventy years (1830–1900).[69]

It was no accident that blackface entertainment dominated the American stage during this period. At a time when slavery and race were main issues in the country, minstrels provided an antidote for some deep-seated racial and sociological problems. Minstrelsy, with its negative stereotypical image of Blacks, emphasized the differences between Blacks and Whites, differences that assured the White "common" man of his identity and status.[70]

In addition to establishing Blacks in show business, minstrelsy provided theatrical experience for a generation of Black entertainers who could not have received this essential training from another source. Nonetheless, despite the theatrical training, Allan Morrison concluded that minstrelsy also performed a disservice:

> Minstrelsy left a damaging imprint on entertainment in the United States because it caricatured Negro life and pictured the Negro as an irresponsible, grinning, banjo-playing and dancing type devoid of dignity and depth. . . . terrible damage had [also] been done to the image of the Negro entertainer: he had been forced to don a mask decreed by white society. . . . For nearly a century, Negro entertainers strove to rid themselves of the stigma symbolized by the mask they had to wear.[71]

Except as comic relief, there was little interest by White playwrights in Blacks as dramatic material until just before the Civil War. The emotional and moral issue of slavery prompted Harriet Beecher Stowe to write the novel *Uncle Tom's Cabin* (1852). Six months after publication, without Stowe's permission, the novel was adapted by George L. Aiken into a play.[72] Blacks and the conflicts of slavery were brought to the American stage.

Besides minstrelsy, *Uncle Tom's Cabin* (1853), one of the most popular plays of the mid-nineteenth century, provided one of the earliest opportunities for Blacks to appear on the legitimate stage.[73] The way in which the Black woman was depicted in the drama of the Civil War period was directly related to the way in which she was viewed in American culture. The prototype female character of this era was Topsy in *Uncle Tom's Cabin*. "George L. Aiken, adapter of the best-known version of *Uncle Tom's Cabin*, heightened the sentimentality and the melodrama," wrote Loften Mitchell. "His treatment of the character Topsy lacked Mrs. Stowe's understanding and it was, in fact, close to blackface minstrelsy."[74] The stock character (such as Topsy), whose purpose was to authenticate scenes, create atmosphere and comedy, or provide contrast to the virtues and vices of White characters, helped to establish a pattern for the portrayal of African-American women on the stage.

In the period after the Civil War, *Uncle Tom's Cabin* was possibly the most frequently produced play in America. The show was so successful that touring companies called "Tommers" or "Tom Shows" traveled throughout the country presenting versions of *Uncle Tom's Cabin*. In the 1870s Tommer troupes began to incorporate material from minstrel shows, as well as novelties and their own special features (including Black spirituals and up to 100 jubilee singers), in the productions.[75] Ironically, even though *Uncle Tom's Cabin* depicted the stereotypical "Stage Negro," by the late 1870s, "Tom troupes were the only racially integrated shows in the country."[76]

The first production of *Uncle Tom's Cabin* was presented in 1853, but interestingly it was not until 1879 that a Black woman is recorded to have performed the part of Topsy.[77] Up to 1890, because of Topsy and "darky" or "plantation" roles, productions of *Uncle Tom's Cabin* were the only shows (except for specialty acts) in which Black women were seen.[78] By the Nineties, Black jubilee singers and Black specialty acts had become the major attractions for Tommers. By this time, *Uncle Tom's Cabin* bore little resemblance to the original play. It was, in fact, closely related to minstrels, which White audiences enjoyed.[79]

Nevertheless, even these productions, in which the role of the Black woman was cast, set, and stereotyped, provided opportunities for the Black female performer to develop and expand her stage image: "According to a note in the *New York Dramatic Mirror* in 1890 'Uncle Tom's Cabin* is playing in the English provinces with a ballet of negro girls. They dress entirely in black and send the audience home feeling

as though they attended a funeral.' By 1892 Topsy, played by Jennie
Chapman, was introducing 'several clever breakdowns'; and by 1899 the
drama was graced by a Cake-Walk."[80]

By 1890 many Black parents had been able to educate their children.
There were educated poets, songwriters, musicians, and singers among
other skilled and talented artists and professionals. Many of them
played a significant role in developing show business into the large in-
dustry it has become today.[81] Edith Isaacs called the years 1890–1917
"The Middle Distance."[82] Not only had Blacks begun to be accepted as
subject matter for the legitimate stage, but they had received limited
access to the theatre, both as audience and artists. Isaacs noted the
important contributions which African-American artists made to the
theatre during this time: "Not much is left in actual performance of
the things that were then most popular, but, on the other hand, almost
everything that Negro theatre artists and musicians are doing today
had its beginnings in the Middle Distance and much of what our theatres and concert halls and radio, and most of what our night clubs are
doing had its source or its flood-tide here."[83]

The first significant challenge to the blackface minstrel tradition occurred in 1890 with the appearance of *The Creole Show*. "*The Creole
Show* ... featured girls for the first time in a major minstrel," noted
Nathan Huggins. "They were lightskinned dancers whose dance and
burlesque accommodated the style of the 'olio' to standard variety
acts."[84] The popularity of *The Creole Show* paved the way for a succes-
sion of successful non-blackface, all-Black musicals produced between
1890 and 1912. They included *The Octoroon, Oriental American, In Dahomey*, and *The Red Moon*, to name a few. "The success of these shows,"
wrote Langston Hughes, "led at the turn of the century to the great era
of Negro musical comedy in which not only performers but black composers and writers gained a foothold in the commercial theater, and
beauty became a part of the brown-skinned world of make-believe."[85]

Between 1890 and 1910 Daniel and Charles Frohman, managers of
Proctor's 23rd Street Theatre; Steele MacKaye of the Madison Square
Garden Theatre; Albert Marshall Palmer (Palmer's Theatre); Lester
Wallack of Wallack's Theatre; and Augustin Daly were among the most
powerful men in American theatre.[86] During this period the impact of
economics produced major changes in the American theatre. Around
1890 a small group of businessmen, whose primary interest was profit,
emerged to control theatres, production, and booking. During the early
Nineties, Abraham L. Erlanger and Marc Klaw controlled several theatres in important cities and had 200 exclusive bookings in one-night
stands in the Southwest; Charles Frohman and Al Hayman controlled
300 theatres in the West. In 1896 Klaw and Erlanger and Frohman and

Hayman joined Samuel F. Nixon and Frederick Zimmerman, who controlled Philadelphia and the surrounding area, to form the Theatrical Syndicate. Because of the demand for a centralized form of booking created by the combination company (a touring troupe consisting of a star and full company, complete with scenery and properties), the Syndicate, and later Sam, Lee, and J. J. Shubert, achieved a monopoly of the theatre business.[87]

The Syndicate offered a full season of star attractions on condition that local managers booked exclusively through them. Those who refused were eliminated. The Syndicate held key routes between large cities and unless productions could play along the way, touring was financially impossible. Through control of the booking business, by 1900 American theatre was controlled by the Syndicate.[88] Since the Syndicate refused to accept plays not likely to appeal to a large audience, Black productions were especially vulnerable.

By 1907 the competition between the Syndicate and the Shuberts had resulted in having more theatres than either organization could fill. In 1913 the Syndicate, which was breaking up, and the Shuberts came to an agreement to regulate competition in Boston, Chicago, St.Louis, and Philadelphia. In some instances, they even booked through each other. Between 1900 and 1915, American theatre became a business venture and was dominated by commercial interests.[89] Because of this profit-motive development, commercial theatre became less accessible to Blacks.

Only Black stars such as Williams and Walker and Johnson and Dean played the Northern White circuit. Most Black entertainers toured the South, playing in carnivals, minstrels, and circuses.[90] In 1913 Black comedian Sherman H. Dudley began to lease theatres in Washington, D.C. By 1920 he had helped to organize a Black vaudeville circuit called T.O.B.A., the Theatre Owners' Booking Association (frequently nicknamed "Tough on Black Artists").[91] Composed of both Black and White theatre owners, T.O.B.A. was also known as "the Chitlin' Circuit."[92]

The 1890 federal census listed 1,490 Black "actors and showmen;" however, none was performing in legitimate drama.[93] By 1894 that number had increased sharply. During the same year, 2,000 Blacks responded to an ad in the *New York Clipper* (the major theatrical newspaper of the nineteenth century) for forty openings in Black minstrels.[94] The New York *Dramatic Mirror* and the *Indianapolis Freeman*, a Black newspaper, also ran theatrical advertisements. Fletcher recalled that those of the Harrison brothers were most provocative: "WANTED: Colored performers, men and women. Men who can double in band and orchestra or band and stage. Real black men and yellow women. Do not worry about your parade outfits because they are furnished by the company [c. 1890–1900]."[95]

As conditions for Blacks began to worsen, particularly in the South, more and more Blacks migrated to the Northern cities. This increase in Black population "disturbed and threatened Northern white men, who feared that their jobs and their women would be lost to the black 'intruder.' "[96] As Harlem changed from a White suburb to a Black ghetto, the fear of the "intermingling of the races" intensified. Such bias resurfaced "when Negro stars emerged," noted Robert Toll, "stars who seemed to represent the first evidence that black people would no longer remain content with inferior positions."[97]

In 1900 a riot broke out in New York after a Black man killed a White policeman. In retaliation, White mobs, with the approval of the police, decimated the Black community. "At the height of these disturbances," wrote Morrison, "cries were heard 'get Ernest Hogan and Williams and Walker, Cole and Johnson.' These were names of famous Negroes in show business whom the crowds knew and regarded as symbols of the Negro community."[98] During the riot, Ernest Hogan was badly beaten and George Walker escaped injury only by hiding in a cellar all night.[99]

As racial tensions increased, Black progress in show business decreased, indicating a connection between artistic development and social and cultural restrictions.[100] A number of Black entertainers escaped and profited by touring and living abroad. They performed in Russia, Germany, England, France, Japan, China, Australia, Hungary, and Austria. These men and women epitomized the "pioneering presence of black performers who literally spread throughout the world."[101] This exodus did not stop until World War I.

By 1910 the number of professional Black entertainers had risen to 3,088; most were appearing in all-Black musicals.[102] After 1910, however, Black involvement in professional theatre in New York nearly came to a halt. By that time, George Walker, Bob Cole, and Ernest Hogan had left show business due to illness. Also in 1910, Bert Williams signed with the *Ziegfeld Follies*. Without these stars to assure the success of a production, White producers and theatre managers withdrew their backing from Black musical shows. Unfortunately, the leadership of these men left no producer/performer teams to develop Black musical comedy. So, from 1912 to 1917, except for Bert Williams, Blacks did not perform on the Broadway stage.

Nonetheless, during this absence from Broadway, an aggressive effort developed by Black artists and others to establish a theatre in the Black community. This venture produced, in 1915, Harlem's first community theatre company, the Lafayette Players. The Lafayette Players were well received, presenting Black casts performing Broadway standards such as Alexandre Dumas's *The Count of Monte Cristo* and *The Three Musketeers;* Dion Boucicault's *The Octoroon;* and Bayard Veiller's *Within the Law;* as well as Goethe's *Faust* and Molière's *The Follies of Scapin.*[103]

Establishing an ethnic theatre during this period was very difficult for Blacks since "their entertainment was tailored to the standards of mass culture."[104] Just as theatre artists and technicians require training, an audience must also be educated to support such a theatre. Because of the pioneering efforts of the Lafayette Players, "Black audiences saw, for the first time, Black entertainers performing in a medium that differed greatly from the usual minstrel-type comedy with which audiences were familiar."[105] Unfortunately, the progress of Black playwrights did not keep pace with that of Black performers. No serious drama by and about Blacks was ever put on at the Lafayette. Like minstrelsy, however, this move from Broadway to Harlem provided another training ground for Black actors to sharpen their skills. They would soon be thrust onto the mainstream professional stage once again.

On 5 April 1917, three *dramatic* plays were presented by the Colored Players at the Garden Theatre in Madison Square Garden in New York City.[106] Collectively entitled *Three Plays for a Negro Theatre,* these plays challenged the traditional portrayals of Blacks on the stage and their historical stereotypes. Written by a White author (and produced and directed by Whites), these plays represented the "first serious attempt to depict the Negro from his own point of view," commented Carl Van Vechten. "The Negro dramatist," he added, "has no desire to remind himself or his prospective audiences of the dark days and unpleasant traditions, which he thinks best forgotten."[107] Speaking of this period and the future of Black theatre, Van Vechten lamented,

> it is doubtful if Negro audiences would go in large numbers to see a characteristic Negro play, the musical play excepted. Negroes as a whole are astonishingly lacking in race pride. Many of them have succumbed to the effect of white domination: they were ashamed of their race. . . . I am afraid there will never be a Negro theatre, and if there is one I am sure it will appeal more to whites than to blacks.[108]

Some of Van Vechten's observations were valid in 1917, made prior to significant changes in the social and cultural status of Blacks in America. At the time, conditions for Blacks were very bleak, and Van Vechten could not have predicted either the feelings of ethnic pride aroused by the Marcus Garvey Movement or the cultural advancements achieved during the Harlem Renaissance of the 1920s.

A few Blacks had been writing serious plays before the 1920s. W.E.B. Du Bois and others, including Van Vechten, began a concerted effort to develop a Black theatre. The spread of the Little Theatre Movement and the initiation of the *Crisis* (1925) and *Opportunity* (1925) literary contests, sponsored by the NAACP and the National Urban League, respectively, coupled with a shift in attitude and thought of both Blacks and Whites, provided encouragement as well as opportunity for Black playwrights to gain experience, exposure, and training. With the new Black Drama, however, came the Black playwright's dilemma: "the Black playwright was faced with having to choose between pleasing the overwhelmingly white audience of the commercial theatre or writing for a Black audience, which wished to see its image with less distortion, but could not provide a commensurate material reward."[109]

With the emergence of the Black playwright also came discussion about what would constitute a Black theatre. In a 1926 *Crisis* article, Du Bois theorized:

> The plays of a Negro must be: 1. About us. That is, they must have plots which reveal Negro life as it is. 2. By us. That is, they must be written by Negro authors who understand from birth and continued association just what it means to be a Negro today. 3. For us. That is, the theatre must cater primarily to Negro audiences and be supported and sustained by their entertainment and approval. 4. Near us. The theatre must be in a Negro neighborhood near the mass of ordinary Negro people.[110]

The Black playwright's dilemma is still not reconciled today. Seventy years after Van Vechten's erroneous predictions, however, there is a Black theatre in America, with New York being its largest producing center. Furthermore, as Du Bois had visualized sixty years earlier, today's Black theatre is sustained by the plays of Black writers who depict a wide range of the Black experience. Black theatre, like all theatre, is faced with the problem of obtaining adequate financing. Nevertheless, there is an aggressive effort by Black artists and Black communities, with the help of interested Whites, to sustain Black theatre across America. Black drama has also evolved into a field of study including history, theory, and criticism.

The turn-of-the-century American theatre reflected the tastes of the people. Characterized by the attitudes of a changing society, this transitional period provided the setting for nearly three decades of productivity for Black theatre-artists, especially women. During this era, major changes occurred in the portrayal of the Black character and in the development of the Black performer. The progression from minstrelsy to musicals to drama signaled a new era of Black involvement in American theatre. Moreover, those Black women who launched their careers during this time played a significant role in furthering the acceptance of Black entertainers worldwide. It was also during this brief but pivotal period that the Black dramatic actress emerged, developed, and began to practice her craft, laying the foundation for the acceptance of the contemporary Black dramatic actress.

1

THE BLACK FEMALE ARTIST
AND THE AMERICAN STAGE
PRIOR TO 1890

By challenging established roles, nineteenth-century Black women created new performing opportunities for themselves. During the early
1850s, anti-aristocratic feelings ran high among the new common-man
audiences. "This was the time," noted Toll, "when raucous, folk-based
entertainment and black-face minstrel songs in Afro-American dialect—not opera—were in vogue in America."[1] Yet during this same
period, when there was no demand for the serious Black singer, Elizabeth Taylor-Greenfield debuted on the American concert stage. Born a
slave in 1809 in Natchez, Mississippi (of an African father and an In-
dian/White mother), but raised in freedom, Elizabeth Taylor-Greenfield
became "the first American Negro musician to gain recognition in England and Canada as well as the United States."[2]

Brought to Philadelphia at the age of one by a Quaker, Mrs. Greenfield, Elizabeth's musical talents were encouraged at an early age. In
1844 her patron died, leaving her a substantial inheritance. The will
was contested, however.[3] Long before Mrs. Greenfield's death, Elizabeth had acquired "celebrity status" in her limited circle, singing at various benefits and charities. Unable to get professional training because
"no money would induce a 'Professor' to include a 'Darkie' among his
pupils," Elizabeth taught herself to play the guitar. The turning point
in her singing career occurred when Miss Price, a talented musician
and daughter of a Philadelphia physician, heard of Elizabeth and offered to accompany her on piano. Later, Miss Price taught her to play
the piano.[4]

Shortly after her mistress's death, Elizabeth, who had little money, traveled to Buffalo, New York, to be with relatives and friends. While in Buffalo she received the patronage of a wealthy philanthropist, the wife of General Potter, who encouraged her to seek a professional singing career. Through the efforts of her generous patron, Elizabeth gave several private concerts for the city's elite. In the early part of 1852, she made her first public appearance. Her program included "On the Banks of the Guadalquivir," "Home, Sweet Home," and the drinking song from *Lucrezia Borgia.* Some patrons came due to the novelty of a Black woman giving a concert. Such was her success, however, that the press likened her voice to Jenny Lind and Parodi, and bestowed the so-briquet "The Black Swan" upon her.[5] The *Buffalo Express* said:

> She now reads the most difficult music with a readiness and precision that would do credit to a finished master, and possesses a power and cultivation of voice that surprises and confounds the listener. . . . Give the Black Swan the cultivation and experience of the fair Swede, or Madlle. Parodi, and she will rank favorable with those popular singers who have carried the nation into captivity by their rare musical abilities.[6]

From Buffalo, Greenfield went to Rochester, New York, at the invitation of its citizens. "Jenny Lind," reported the *Rochester Paper,* "has never drawn a better house as to character, than that which listened with evident satisfaction to this unheralded and almost unknown African Nightingale."[7] Afterward she traveled to Canada, New England, Maryland, Pennsylvania, and Ohio. The *Cincinnati Enquirer* raved: "In compass, her voice is the most extraordinary we have ever heard being fully satisfied that it possesses the astonishing range of 27 notes."[8] The Springfield, Massachusetts, *Post* went so far as to predict that she "will yet win a fame scarcely second to any cantatrice in the world."[9]

On 31 March 1853, immediately before departing for Europe, she performed in New York City at the Metropolitan Hall before an audience of 4000. This was the same theatre where Anna Bishop, Henrietta Sontag, Jenny Lind, and Parodi had appeared.[10] One reviewer wrote: "Miss Greenfield's reception was very favorable, though occasionally the applause was mingled with ill-mannered laughter, from certain individuals who were more nice in colour than in those of tone." He commented that "the Swan, who is a stout, good-looking coloured woman, . . . received her bouquets and frequent encores with a propriety of demeanor that operated decidedly in her favor."[11]

During the 1853–54 season in New York City, *Uncle Tom's Cabin* ran for an unprecedented 325 consecutive performances.[12] This moving, sentimental melodrama provoked increasing controversy over the emotional and moral issue of slavery. Due to intensified anti-Black feelings, there had been speculations that Greenfield's appearance might cause trouble. In fact, "a very large posse of police was in attendance in the hall." There were no disturbances, however.[13]

Greenfield sang before an all-White audience. Blacks were barred from the Metropolitan Hall. She was aware of this condition, but, like many others who would come after her, Greenfield was confronted with the Black performer's dilemma: She had to decide whether, in order to earn a living and to get the proper professional exposure, to appear where her people were not permitted. Due to the problems of race relations, the Black performer's dilemma is still not reconciled today.

Frederick Douglass, the noted ex-slave, abolitionist, and orator, criticized Greenfield severely for her decision. He felt that by compromising, she was not only accepting discrimination but also "betraying her people." In an editorial in *The North Star,* his weekly anti-slavery paper, Douglass told his readers: "She should be called no longer the Black Swan, but the White Raven."[14]

On March 30, the day before the concert, a group of Black clergymen sent Greenfield a letter reminding her that they "and their numerous coloured friends in the city are denied the privilege of attending" the concert at Metropolitan Hall. "That they not be left with the present painful impression," they respectfully requested she repeat her "concert on Monday evening, the 4th of April, at the Broadway Tabernacle." They added, if repeated, the concert "will be public, and that no one shall be excluded who complies with the terms."[15]

These men also suggested "that the proceeds, after paying expenses, be divided between the Home for Aged Coloured persons and the Coloured Orphan Asylum." Greenfield wrote back saying, "I will with pleasure sing for the benefit of any charity that will elevate the condition of my coloured brethren."[16] Before departing for London on April 6, she gave a second concert for this group of citizens.[17]

With Greenfield's help, these New York City Blacks were able to circumvent some of the restrictions imposed upon them. Even though she was admired and applauded by the city's elite, Greenfield also felt the sting of racial prejudice. While in Buffalo, she had been befriended by Madame Marietta Alboni, who gave her much advice. While Greenfield was in New York, some of her friends tried to secure a private box for the Italian Opera at Niblo's Gardens so she could hear Madame Alboni sing—they were denied.[18]

After touring the Northern states, aided by the citizens of Buffalo, Greenfield went to Europe to study and perform. She arrived in London on 18 April 1853. When promised arrangements left her stranded she was aided by Harriet Beecher Stowe, who was in London. Stowe's

Uncle Tom's Cabin had been staged, widely read, and had sold 300,000 copies in England and on the Continent. Greenfield achieved immediate success. The London *Times, Observer,* and *Morning Post* gave glowing reviews of her concerts. On 10 May 1854 she gave a command performance at Buckingham Palace for Queen Victoria. Despite her accomplishment, Greenfield's plans to study abroad for three years did not materialize. In July of 1854, she returned to the United States. Shortly afterward, she gave a concert in New York City. The *New York Herald* said: " 'The Swan' sings now in true artistic style, and the wonderful powers of her voice have been developed by good training."[19] Greenfield returned to Philadelphia where she taught voice and gave occasional concerts. On 31 March 1876, the Black Swan died suddenly of paralysis in her home.[20]

Though she gained substantial success at the beginning of her career, Elizabeth Taylor-Greenfield was not permitted the opportunity to fulfill the promise of her talents. Nonetheless, her pioneering efforts paved the way for the acceptance of Marie Selika, Sissieretta Jones, and other Black women concert singers who received considerable recognition both here and abroad. Moreover, as we will see, she began a tradition that provided an entrée to the legitimate stage for Black women.

Greenfield appeared on the stage before either of the Hyers Sisters was born. Yet, just thirteen years after Greenfield had achieved recognition, Anna Madah Hyers (b. 1855) and Emma Louise Hyers (b. 1857) launched their careers on the professional concert stage.[21] Such was their creative passion and genius that during 1876, the same year of Greenfield's death, they began producing and performing in Black theatricals. Because of their popularity and initiative in making the transition to the theatre, the Hyers Sisters became the first Black women to gain success on the American stage.

Their parents, Sam B. and Annie E. Hyers, migrated from New York (when Anna was a year old) to Sacramento, California, in 1856. Emma was born the following year. These sisters demonstrated their musical talents early and studied music with their parents, who were amateur musicians.[22] They were considered musical prodigies. Unlike Elizabeth Greenfield (who had to go to Europe to receive training), when Anna was seven and Emma nine they were placed with the German instructor Hugo Sank, where they studied voice, piano, and language. Later they studied with opera singer Josephine d'Ormy. Anna, a soprano, and Emma, a contralto, debuted on 22 April 1867 before an audience of 800 at the Metropolitan Theatre in Sacramento. Their program included "Casta Diva" and Verdi's "Forse' lui chi l'anima." The press commented on the purity and sweetness of Madah's voice and Emma's fine contralto.[23]

After years of further study, insisted upon by their father, the Hyers Sisters undertook an extended tour of the country, traveling from West to East. On 12 August 1871, assisted by a baritone named LeCount and their father, they appeared at the Salt Lake City Theatre. The first part of the concert consisted of selections from the first and second acts of Donizetti's opera *Linda di Chamounix*. During the Western part of the tour, the Missouri, Illinois, and Ohio papers praised the singers. "Anna's singing of E flat above the staff with the greatest of ease, and her bird-like trills, caused her to be likened to Jenny Lind, while Emma's voice was said to be one of remarkable quality and richness 'rarely heard.' "[24]

For concerts in New England and New York, their father engaged noted baritone John Luca; rising tenor of the day, Wallace King; and accompanist A. C. Taylor. Their program consisted mainly of operatic arias, duos, trios, and quartets.[25] The group gave concerts at the Young Men's Christian Association Hall in Brooklyn and at Steinway Hall in New York City. They were well received by full houses of cultured patrons, and the press was flattering. The New York *Tribune* reported: "These are two young colored girls who have received a musical training in California, and who are by no means 'Jubilee' singers, as the program of last evening clearly shows."[26] Of their voices, the reviewer for the New York *Evening Post* wrote: "Miss Anna Hyers possesses a flexible voice of great compass, clear and steady in the higher notes. Miss Emma, contralto, has a voice of great power and depth; qualities which, in impassioned strains give it a richness not often heard in chamber concerts."[27]

After appearing in Boston, where they sang before Patrick S. Gilmore and Eben Tourgee (who became director of the New England Conservatory of Music), the ensemble won critical acclaim performing throughout the area. The Worcester *Daily Press* raved: "the quartette singing was unaccompanied, and was the finest that has been heard in this city for years. The voices blended beautifully, and were full of expression."[28]

The Hyers Sisters remained in Boston in order to continue their musical training. In 1872 they were invited to sing at P. S. Gilmore's World Jubilee in Boston. By 1875 they had organized a small concert company and were performing primarily in New England.[29] For their concerts at the Boston Theatre, where they appeared in Sunday night "sacred" concerts, they were supported by a forty-piece orchestra conducted by the White orchestra leader Napier Lothian. Their success at these engagements added to their growing fame. At one performance, the audience insisted upon thirteen encores.[30]

As early as 1876 their father, who was also their business manager, enlarged the company in order to produce drama.[31] The troupe, now called "The Hyers Sisters Musical Company, Starring Sam Lucas," gave as its first production *Out of Bondage; or, Before and After the War* (1876), which featured Lucas in the role of Mischievous Henry, his first big hit. It appears that *Out of Bondage* was the first musical show to be produced by a Black organization.[32] Coauthored with White writer Rev. Joseph Bradford of Boston, this comedy depicts "the Darky as he existed in Ante-Bellum Days, showing his humorous characteristics without burlesque. Introducing Musical Novelties and the Old-Time Southern Camp-Meeting and Jubilee Melodies." Emma played Kalooah and Anna was Narcisse, Pet of the Plantation.[33] Rounding out the piece by performing their "specialty," "the final act takes the form of a concert during which the sisters sing selections from their regular repertoire."[34] *Out of Bondage* made history: it signaled the beginning of the transition from minstrelsy to Black musical comedy.[35]

In addition to *Princess Orelia of Madagascar* (c. 1877), which they wrote, the Hyers Sisters added Black playwright Pauline E. Hopkin's *Urlina, the African Princess* and *The Underground Railroad* to their repertory.[36] The sisters first performed *Urlina, the African Princess* in 1879 at the Bush Theatre in San Francisco.

> Called an "operatic bouffe extravaganza," . . . plot is laid in Africa, where a usurping king has banished the princess Urlina, rightful successor to the throne. But the usurper's son, prince Zurleska, sees a picture of the princess, falls in love with her, and sets out with his ally Kekolah to rescue her and her maid. However, as the young people return to the kingdom they are seized by the king's soldiers, imprisoned, and left to starve to death. Kekolah escapes, disguises himself as a traveller, and with the help of his friends succeeds in freeing the prisoners and overthrowing the usurper.[37]

After playing in San Francisco, they moved *Urlina* to New Market, Oregon. Though it was enthusiastically received, according to the critic reviewing the production, "the real gem of the evening was the Midnight Quartet from *Martha* which was sung by the Hyers sisters, John Luca and Wallace King."[38] By presenting *Urlina, the African Princess,* the Hyers Sisters became the "first black theatre company to stage a musical set in Africa, a trend that will be followed by Cole and Johnson, Williams and Walker, and other notable black companies in later years."[39]

The Hyers Sisters toured extensively, primarily in the West, with these plays under the sponsorship of the Redpath Lyceum Bureau. Critics praised the group as being "one of the best opera-bouffe troupes in America." Over the years, the company included pianist-composer Jacob Sawyer, Mrs. Francis A. Powell, Billy Kersands, Dora S. King, Grace V. Overall, pianist Celestine O. Browne, and Sam Lucas.[40]

Early in 1883 the Hyers's dramatic troupe disbanded temporarily. In May of that year, they reorganized the concert company and appeared in the Callendar Consolidated Spectacular Minstrel Festival in July at the Grand Opera House in New York before touring nationwide. Gustave and Charles Frohman, the White owners of the show, planned to form a Colored Opera Troupe starring the Hyers Sisters in the Fall of 1883. The company was to feature Marie Selika and her husband, Sampson Williams, a chorus, and an orchestra of forty. These plans, however, never materialized.[41]

By the Fall of 1886, the Hyerses had reorganized their dramatic company and were touring with *Out of Bondage,* starring Sam Lucas as Mischievous Henry, the role he had created in 1876.[42] They also presented *Out of Bondage* in February 1890. However, Sam Lucas was not in the company. The other principal female part (Aunt Naoma) was played by a Miss Bradford. Providing work for other performers, the cast also included Field Hands, Cotton Pickers, and Jubilee Singers.[43] During 1891 the Hyers Sisters were playing the East with *Out of Bondage, Colored Aristocracy,* and *Blackville Twins.*[44]

During the early 1890s, their names appeared less frequently in the press. An April 1893 press notice announced that they were leaving the stage and would appear only for special engagements. Thereafter, no press notices of the Hyerses as a duo appeared. In 1894 Emma performed with an *Uncle Tom's Cabin* company, and in 1894 Anna joined John Isham's *Octoroons,* singing in the operatic finale called "Thirty Minutes Around the Operas." Sometime before 1900 Emma died.[45]

During the 1899–1900 season, Anna toured Australia with Curtis' Afro-American Minstrel Company, which also included Ernest Hogan and Billy McClain.[46] The 12 July 1899 issue of *The Referee,* Sidney, reported: "Miss Madah Anna Hyers, 'The Bronze Patti,' was heard to great advantage in a couple of operatic selections."[47] After returning to the United States, Anna performed with various Isham companies until 1902 when she retired from the stage.[48] Later, Anna married Dr. Robert J. Fletcher of Sacramento where she settled. In 1920 she was still alive, living quietly, but actively involved in music in the church.[49] The date of Anna's death has not been established.

Debuting on the professional concert stage just two years after the Civil War, the Hyers Sisters demonstrated "to the country at large that black artists – and by extrapolation all black people – could be equal to whites in any field of endeavor," contended Hill.[50] In the face of tremendous obstacles, they made significant contributions. By shattering the traditional stage image of Black women, they provided a new image for the entry of the Black female performer on the professional stage in America. Moreover, through their talents and innovative ideas, they provided the foundation that would eventually lead to the evolution of Black musical comedy into the form we know it as today. The magnitude of their accomplishments cannot be overstated. As Hill put it: "They were, in fact, the precursors of black musical theatre in America."[51]

An interesting figure in the musical life of Boston was Mrs. Arianna Cooley Sparrow. The daughter of the quadroon whom Harriet Beecher Stowe depicted as one of the characters in *Uncle Tom's Cabin*, she sang in the Tremont Temple Choir. Later she was a soprano for the Berkeley Street Quartet. She was a member of the Handel and Haydn Society for a number of years. Due to excellent training under the well-known teacher H. L. Whitney, Mrs. Sparrow continued to sing at St. Augustine Episcopal Church in Boston when she was over eighty.[52]

The most famous Black prima donna of the 1880s was Mme. Marie Selika (Mrs. Sampson Williams). Born c. 1849 in Natchez, Mississippi, she was taken to Cincinnati as an infant. While there, a wealthy family heard her sing and arranged for her to study professionally. About 1874 she went to San Francisco, California, where she studied with Signora G. Bianchi, and debuted there in 1876. After a year of further study with a Mr. Farinin in Chicago, she began giving concerts in the East in 1878. At her 1878 Philadelphia debut, the soubriquet "Queen of Staccata" was bestowed upon her when she sang the "Staccato Polka."[53]

Her stage name, "Selika," was taken from the heroine of Meyerbeer's opera *L'Africaine.* In 1880, while under the management of Lt. William Dupree, she gave several concerts. "She created a furore [sic] by her marvelous coloratura singing," wrote Maude Cuney-Hare.[54] In 1882 she traveled to Europe with her husband, an aspiring baritone known as "Vilaski," where she gained international fame.[55] The Paris *Figaro* wrote: "Madame Selika sang in great style. She has a very strong voice of depth and compass, rising with perfect ease from C to C, and she trills like a feathered songster. Her range is marvelous and her execution and style of rendition show perfect cultivation. Her 'Echo Song' cannot be surpassed. It was beyond criticism. It was an artistic triumph."[56]

Of her performance in Berlin, the reviewer for the *Tagblatt* said:

Mme. Selika with her singing roused the audience to the highest pitch of enthusiasm, after her first aria, she was twice recalled, and could quiet the vociferous applause only by rendering a selection with orchestral accompaniment. . . . With her pure tones, her wonderful trills and roulades, her correct rendering of the most difficult intervals, she not only gains the admiration of amateurs but also that of professional musicians and critics.[57]

In October of 1883 she sang at a command performance for Queen Victoria.[58]

Mme. Selika returned to America in 1885. Soon afterward, she and her husband (who was also known as the Hawaiian Baritone) toured extensively across the country. Between 1887 and 1892 she made her second tour of Europe and the West Indies. Around 1893 Mme. Selika and her husband settled in Cleveland, Ohio, where she headed a voice studio and they continued to tour. During this time, she managed her own career.[59] "Despite problems of management," noted Eileen Southern, "she sang all over the nation and was regarded as the leading prima donna of the race during the time."[60]

During the late 1890s, after a number of successful years on the concert stage, "critics began to compare her unfavorably to younger singers – Flora Batson and Sissieretta Jones, for example – and her career began to languish."[61] Around 1911, after her husband's death, Mme. Selika moved to New York City where she taught voice for several years at the Martin-Smith School of Music in Harlem. In 1919 she was honored at a testimonial concert given by the New York Black music establishment. Mme. Selika taught privately until 1936. She died in 1937 at the age of eighty-seven.[62]

The DeWolf Sisters, Sadie and Rosa, were singers of exceptional merit. Born in Charlotte, North Carolina, they came to Boston where they sang with the "Walker Quintet" and in Sunday night concerts. During the 1880s, they were members of the Sam Lucas Concert Company of Boston.[63]

Sadie, a soprano, and Rosa, a contralto, were heard on the vaudeville circuit for two years before joining Sam T. Jack's *The Creole Show* on 4 August 1890.[64] The original cast of *Black Patti's Troubadours* (1896) also included the DeWolf Sisters.[65] Shortly after 1902, according to Cuney-Hare, "the sisters retired after twelve years' stage experience in a refined type of vaudeville that would illy fit the coarse acts which gradually found a wide public."[66] On 23 May 1917, Rosa DeWolf died in Boston.[67] The date of Sadie's death is not available.

A younger singer, Flora Batson, born in Providence, Rhode Island, in 1870, possessed a remarkable soprano voice. As a ballad singer, she toured throughout America, New Zealand, Australia, and Africa. In 1887 she formed a concert company, and on 21 March of that year, she appeared at the Music Hall in Boston. Acclaimed for her performance, "she became popular on southern tours for her high class entertainment." For three months she sang as a soloist at a large temperance revival in New York. At the height of her career she married a White businessman, James Berger, who was also her business manager. On 2 December 1906, Flora Batson died suddenly in Philadelphia.[68]

As demonstrated by the demise of the African Company, Blacks performing in drama were not accepted by the White theatrical establishment. In an attempt to circumvent these restrictions, as with the African Theatre, late nineteenth-century Blacks formed their own companies and established their own theatres. A number of Black drama groups sprang up in urban centers throughout the country. During the last two decades of this century, Providence, Louisville, and Baltimore had two companies each. Philadelphia, San Francisco, and the District of Columbia had three; Chicago had four; and New York had at least ten. Unlike the touring Black professionals, these amateurs and semi-professionals presented dramatic productions as opposed to vaudeville, minstrels, and variety shows.[69]

The most distinguished group performing drama during this time was the Astor Place Company of Colored Tragedians in New York. In 1878 Benjamin J. Ford, a waiter, and his wife, Hattie E. Hill, presented *Richard III* at the Lyric Theatre on Sixth Avenue. By 1884 they were rehearsing at the Grand Central Theatre on Astor Place, near Broadway. On 12 June 1864 they presented *Othello* at the Brooklyn Atheneum for an audience of 300.[70] Of this performance Errol Hill concluded that

> Ford looked the part of the Moor, but his performance was disappointing; he lacked passion and his diction was faulty. Hattie Hill did not appear in this production. They must have quarreled and were still not reconciled in September of that year, at which time she denied in a press report that she was engaged to perform with Ford in John Banim's tragedy *Damon and Pythias* and in *Richard III*. The new leading lady was Alice Brooks, an octoroon who made a pretty and pleasing, if inexperienced, Desdemona.[71]

Of the Blacks performing drama during the nineteenth century, none was more prominent than Henrietta Vinton Davis. Born in Baltimore, Maryland, but raised in Washington, D.C., Davis, at age fifteen, graduated from a Washington school and took a teaching post in Maryland. By 1878 she was back in Washington working as a secretary in the office of the Recorder of Deeds. She became a student of the well-known elocutionist Miss Marguerita Saxton, and on 25 April 1883 she debuted as a reciter at Marinin's Hall in Washington, D.C. She was introduced by the man for whom she worked in the recorder's office, the Honorable Frederick Douglass.[72]

Davis was advertised as "the first lady of her race to publicly essay a debut in Shakespearean and other legitimate characters." Her program included speeches of Juliet (from *Romeo and Juliet*) and Portia (from *The Merchant of Venice*).[73] "The Associated Press flashed the news throughout the world, and Miss Davis at once took her place among the professional women of the age," wrote Dr. Lawson A. Scruggs in *Women of Distinction* (1893).[74] Local reactions to her performance were glowing. The 21 July 1883 *Washington Bee* reported:

> She came forward and from the time she said her first line to the close of the last sentence, she wrapped the whole audience so close to her that she became a queen of the stage in their eyes. One moment all was serene and quiet, deep pathos, – the next, all was laughter. . . . She is our first American lady leader, she will in due season become our star on the stage of tragedy and drama.[75]

At the end of her first season, she had added speeches of Rosalind from *As You Like It* and Cleopatra from *Anthony and Cleopatra* to her repertoire. Her desire to appear in a full-scale stage production for the following year did not materialize. On 7 May 1884, however, at Ford's Opera House in Washington, D.C., she and Powhatan Beaty performed in scenes from *Macbeth, Richard III,* and *Ingomar.* Davis played Lady Anne, Lady Macbeth, and Parthenia.[76] Praising Davis's work, the 17 May 1884 *New York Globe* recognized the event as historic.

> As Lady Macbeth, Miss Davis displayed wonderful powers of conception. While we failed to discover in her acting the dull, heavy declamatory style complained of by some critics, to me it was plainly apparent that Miss Davis has great reserve dramatic powers, which have not been drawn upon because of the influence that always somehow represses the spontaneous outflow of genius in beginners. . . . The perfect adaptation of Miss Davis to her chosen profession is undisputed. She has earned the plaudits of professional critics, and her success has opened the dramatic door to many. Thus leap by leap the colored man and woman encroach upon the ground so long held sacred by their white brother and sister.[77]

For this performance, the audience was integrated. As with the African Company sixty years earlier, some White patrons found it difficult to accept Black actors in serious roles. The 8 May 1884 *Washington Post* described the atmosphere:

> There were many white people in the house who seemed disposed to turn to comedy the tragic efforts of the actors. In this they were not wholly successful, for the earnestness and intelligence of several of the leading performers were such as to command the respect of those most disposed to find cause for laughter in everything said or done. . . . The scene from *Macbeth* went creditably, all things considered, Miss Davis and Mr. Beaty showing a knowledge of the requirements of the parts which they essayed which, it is safe to say, surprised those in the audience competent to judge.[78]

Also in 1884, she appeared once with the Astor Company in *Damon and Pythias*.[79] During this time, Davis was under the management of Thomas T. Symmons, a "race" man who formed a concert and dramatic company to support her. Over the next nine years she gave recitals throughout the South, East, and West.[80]

Davis settled in Chicago where she taught elocution. In 1893 she was seen in a full-scale dramatic production of William Edgar Easton's *Dessalines* in Chicago. This romantic melodrama depicts the conflict between the freed Blacks and the mulattoes for control of Haiti. Dessalines saves Clarisse, sister of one of the mulatto leaders. In the end the two, who are from different camps, realize they are in love. Davis, who organized the company and produced the play, portrayed Clarisse.[81]

In 1898 Davis appeared in another drama, *Our Old Kentucky Home.* Co-authored by Davis and Black journalist John E. Bruce, this play depicts Clothilde, a Creole slave (acted by Davis), whose courageous efforts help to end the Civil War and unite her with her lover, a freed slave in the Union Army. The play toured throughout the East with some success. Davis continued to perform on the concert stage for five more years. In 1903 she moved back to Washington, D.C. Also in 1903, she revived *Our Old Kentucky Home* in Denver; in 1908 she recited at the Palm Garden in New York; and in 1909 she staged *Dessalines* at the Trinity Congregational Church in Pittsburgh, where she doubled as the comic Dominique and Zingarella, the flower girl. The last play in which Davis appeared was William Easton's *Christophe: A Tragedy.* This piece, also produced by Davis, depicts another Haitian leader's successful slave revolt. *Christophe* opened on 21 March 1912 at the Lenox Casino in New York City, with Davis as Pere L'Avenge and Valerie.[82]

After over thirty years on the stage, Davis gave up performing and became actively involved in politics. By 1919 she had become a director and vice president of Marcus Garvey's Universal Negro Improvement Association (UNIA) and its ill-fated Black Star Line, "one of the cornerstones of Garvey's program for uniting all peoples of African descent." Davis remained a UNIA officer for twelve years, the longest tenure of any member except Garvey. She died at the age of eighty-one in Washington, D.C., in 1941.[83]

Despite incredible odds, Davis's stage career survived only because she refused to quit. Though her talents held much promise, her African ancestry prevented her from being accepted as a serious artist in America. After more than a quarter-century of struggling to achieve an unobtainable goal, it was not surprising that Davis evolved from an artist to an activist. As Errol Hill concluded:

At the height of her powers as a dramatic actress and Shakespeare interpreter, Henrietta Vinton Davis turned from the stage to politics. In so doing, she hoped to gain for black Americans the equality of opportunity that had been denied her in the profession for which she was equipped. Though the Garvey movement failed in its stated objectives, it left a legacy of black self-worth that has continued to fuel demands for a just society. By her dedication to her craft, her achievement as an artist, and her commitment to the improvement of her race, Miss Davis' contribution stands preeminent.[84]

At a time when there was no demand for either serious Black singers or reciters, these women carved out a place for themselves on the American stage. As we have seen, Elizabeth Taylor-Greenfield paved the way for the acceptance of other Black women on the concert stage. We have also seen the Hyers Sisters, the DeWolf Sisters, and Henrietta Vinton Davis continue the evolutionary process of the Black dramatic actress by making the transition from the concert stage to the theatrical stage. By so doing, they helped to lay the foundation for the Black women performers who have followed.

2

GLORIFIED "COLOURED" GIRLS: WOMEN IN TURN-OF-THE-CENTURY BLACK THEATRICALS

From 1879 until 1890, except for "specialty acts," most Black women performers were relegated to playing Topsy and "plantation" roles in *Uncle Tom's Cabin.* In the 1890s, however, with the development of Black musicals such as *The Creole Show,* Black women gained respect and prominence on the American stage.[1] *The Creole Show,* the first musical to challenge successfully the blackface tradition, provided a new image for the Black woman's re-entry (with the earlier entry being the Hyers Sisters in their *Out of Bondage,* c. 1876) to the American stage. The Harlem chronicler James Weldon Johnson stated: "Sam T. Jack, a prominent burlesque-theatre owner and manager, conceived the idea of putting out a Negro show different from anything yet thought of, a show that would glorify the coloured girl."[2]

This production, *The Creole Show,* patterned upon the minstrel show, featured sixteen beautiful Black women who sang and danced, up-to-date material, smart costumes, and the Cakewalk in the finale. It differed from the regular minstrel show "in that the girls were in the centre of the line, with a female interlocutor, and the men on the ends; then came an olio, and then the finale," explained Johnson.[3]

The show was cast in New York, rehearsed in Haverhill, Massachusetts, and opened at the Howard Theatre in Boston before playing New York. The Indianapolis *Freeman* printed this description of *The Creole Show:*

The show commenced with a very pretty first part, attractive grouping of shapely femininity. In "Tropical Revelries," Florence

Brisco was the first conversationalist; Florence Hines, the greatest living female song and dance artist, second and Mrs. Sam Lucas third. The olio sketches were very fine and called for numerous encores. The burlesque, "The Beauty of the Nile, or Doomed by Fire," by William R. Waits, is fine. . . .[4]

In 1891 *The Creole Show* went to Chicago. Later, the cast performed for the entire Summer season during the 1893 Chicago World's Fair at Sam T. Jack's Opera House. Then the show returned to New York, creating a sensation when it opened at the Standard Theatre in Greeley Square, where it ran continuously for five seasons.[5]

The female members of this landmark production included Florence Hines, a popular male impersonator, as the Interlocutor; Sadie and Rosa DeWolfe, classical singers; and Hattie McIntosh, who performed with her husband in their act, "Mr. and Mrs. McIntosh." Stella Wiley (who later married Bob Cole and formed a team known as "Cole and Wiley"), Mattie Wilkes, and Dora Dean were three of the chorus girls.

Although the content of the show appears to have changed a great deal over the years, as late as 1897 *The Creole Show* was still drawing large audiences. During its multiyear run, *The Creole Show* produced a number of female stars: Belle Davis, Mattie Wilkes, Florence Hines, Mazie Brooks, Saddie Jones, and Dora Dean.

Besides the actual production of *The Creole Show* itself, the most significant change initiated by the show was the inclusion of the Cakewalk in the finale. For the first time women were introduced in the dance, ending the all-male minstrel show. From then on all Black shows had women in the company. The Cakewalk, also known as the "Walkaround" and "Chalkline-walk," developed from a "Prize-Walk" (where the prize of a huge cake was awarded the winning couple) performed by slaves at plantation get-togethers.[6]

Cakewalk contests sprang up throughout the country. In addition to providing a form of entertainment, Cakewalk contests offered young, talented Black dancers and singers the opportunity to be seen by prominent people. After such exposure, the top winners usually formed vaudeville and variety acts that were booked throughout the world.[7] The Cakewalk became the first Black dance to be accepted by White society, paving the way for the acceptance of other Black dances.[8] The Cakewalk was a " 'great exhibition dance with such superb theatrical potentialities,' " commented Marian Hannah Winter, " 'that it served as a Negro re-entry permit to the stage.' "[9] As a result of the popularity of the Cakewalk, which stressed individual style and execution, Dora Dean, Ida Forsyne, and Ada Walker became internationally famous performing the dance.

Another departure from the traditional minstrel show occurred in 1895 when John W. Isham, the advance agent for *The Creole Show,* produced *The Octoroons.* This production, a "musical farce" set in New York City, followed the minstrel show pattern, but it too used chorus girls in several specialty numbers in the finale, as well as featuring six of them in principals' parts. "The show closed with a cakewalk jubilee, a military drill, and a 'chorus-march finale.'"[10]

There were seventeen women in the original cast of *The Octoroons.* They included Madame Flowers, Belle Davis, the famous Hyers Sisters, Mattie Wilkes, Hattie McIntosh, Stella Wiley, Mazie Brooks, Grace Holliday, Mamie Emerson, and Ada Overton (who in 1899 became Mrs. George Walker). This was Overton's debut on the professional stage. Receiving international acclaim, she went on to play a prominent role in all of the Williams and Walker productions. By 1897 *The Octoroons* was so successful that three companies were playing throughout the country and one in Great Britain simultaneously.[11]

In 1896 Isham produced *Oriental America.* This musical show, still based on minstrelsy, featured pretty girls and did not end with the traditional "hoe-down," cakewalk, and walk-around. Instead it ended with an operatic medley. The selections included solos and choruses from *Il Trovatore, Faust, Rigoletto, Martha,* and *Carmen. Oriental America* broke further away from the traditional norm by being the first all-Black show to be performed in a legitimate theatre, Palmer's Theatre (later known as Wallack's) rather than in a burlesque house.[12]

Maggie Scott and Desseria Broadley Plato, concert singers; Belle Davis; Ada Walker; Mattie Wilkes; and Inez Clough were among the women performing in the *Oriental America* company. Inez Clough, who sang in the section entitled "Forty Minutes of Grand and Comic Opera," later figured in another event that made theatrical history. Dora Dean, from *The Creole Show,* appeared as a member of the famous quartet that also included Mattie Wilkes, Ollie Burgoyne, and Belle Davis.[13]

The *Morning Times,* Washington, D.C., said of *Oriental America:*

The several scenes in each act have been given the benefit of very attractive and elaborate scenic and electric embellishment and especially is this so in the last act. . . .

Among the many features of the great show were a Japanese dance, cleverly rendered by Fanny Rutledge, Pearl Meredith, Alice Mackey and Carrie Meredith, who sang and danced equally well and were prominent in all the ensemble scenes of the performance. A quartet of cycling girls in bloomers and twentieth century maids, the maids of the Oriental Huzzars, led by Miss Belle

Davis, as well as the hunting scenes and opening chorus form the
"Bells of Cornville." All these and many more were attractive numbers of the performance. Miss Belle Davis gave a pleasing imita-
tion of May Irwin in "I Want You, Ma Honey" and other popular
songs, and Billy Eldridge brought down the house with "Hot Ta-
male Alley" which he sang as it has never been presented here before. A flower ballet by a bevy of pretty girls, assisted by Naby
Ray, was an attractive number in the second act.[14]

With each successful venture, new opportunities for Black women
emerged. A trained concert singer, Madame M. Sissieretta Jones, better known as "Black Patti," in 1896 pioneered with her own company,
"Black Patti's Troubadours." The original "Troubadours" cast included
Stella Wiley and Bob Cole in the comedy sketches; May Bobee, the Creole Nightingale; and thirty chorus girls. Maggie Davis, Ada Overton,
Lena Wise, the DeWolf Sisters, and Madame Reed were also in the
company.[15]

Even though these musicals were based upon minstrelsy, they were
performed on the professional stage and they served to expand on the
minstrel pattern. Like the productions presented by the Hyers Sisters,
these shows gave prominence to the Black woman, and they led up to
the first Black production to break away completely from the minstrel
patter, furthering the movement toward musical comedy as we know it.

The year 1897 marked a turning point in the history of Black theatricals in America. It was then that Bob Cole, an educated actor, singer,
dancer, writer, and composer, joined and eventually headed the first
Black repertory company in New York where Black men and women
could receive formal theatrical training. Composed of twelve to fifteen
members, the All Star Stock Company met and performed at Worth's
Museum, located at Sixth Avenue and 30th Street. Cole was playwright, director, choreographer, and stage manager.[16] The female members of this historic troupe were: Stella Wiley, Willie Farrell (who
performed with her husband in their act "Billy and Willie Farrell"),
Mattie Wilkes, Aline Cassell, and Mamie Flowers.[17]

Several sources reveal the same scant information on this group.
Nevertheless, its existence signified that Blacks were training themselves in anticipation of theatrical careers. Also, because of a later
event, it appears that this company may have been a production/perfor-
mance "workshop" for Cole's future project.

The year 1898 was also pivotal in the development of Black musicals.
Frustrated by the conditions under which Black performers were
forced to work, Bob Cole issued his "Colored Actor's Declaration of Independence of 1898:" "We are going to have our own shows. We are go-

ing to write them ourselves, we are going to have our own stage
managers, our own orchestra leader and our own manager out front to
count up. No divided houses—our race must be seated from the boxes
back."[18] Bob Cole (who had been the stage manager and a comedian
with *The Creole Show*) wrote and staged Black Patti's first musical
show. Unable to reach a financial agreement with her managers, J. Nolan and Rudolph Voelckel, Cole gathered his music together and left.
He was arrested and a court trial followed. Cole declared before the
judge: "These men have amassed a fortune from the product of my
brain, and now they call me a thief; I won't give it up."[19]

Nonetheless, Cole lost the suit, and he had to give up the music. Fortunately, this court dispute prompted him to create a show for himself,
marking a further step in Black theatricals. Cole wrote *A Trip to Coontown* (1898). Though this landmark show "differed little from earlier
black revues," it was the first full-length musical comedy produced, directed, and performed by Blacks.[20] Through determination and defi-
ance, Cole was able to organize his company utilizing the principles of
his "Colored Actor's Declaration of Independence."

After touring in several cities in Canada and in the New York area, on
4 April 1898, *A Trip to Coontown* opened at an out-of-the-way theatre,
Jacob's Third Avenue Theatre (because Cole and any performers who
worked with him had been blacklisted by Nolan and Voelckel).[21] The
critic for the *New York Dramatic Mirror* liked the show:

> The company has not one poor performer among its members.
> The two stars, of course, carried off the honors. Bob Cole as a
> tramp was fully as good as any white comedian whose specialty is
> this style of eccentricity. Billy Johnson as the bunco steerer acted
> with spirit and sang well. . . . Camille Casselle, a very pretty girl,
> was heard to advantage in operatic selections. . . . the Freeman
> Sisters, and the rest of the company lent efficient aid.[22]

Molly Dill, Marguerite Rhodes, Jennie Sheper, Maggie Davis, Estella
Ware, Jennie Hillman, and opera singer Juvia Roan were also in the
cast.[23] Women who performed in the 1899 *Coontown* company included
Mollie Dill, Pauline Freeman, Clara Freeman, Jennie Hillman, Wiletta
Duncan, Pear LaVan, Myrtle Cousins, Alice Mackay, and Edna Alexan-
der.[24]

As more and more Black artists began to perform on stage without
blackface, the blackface makeup of minstrelsy began to give way to the
non-blackface pattern of Black musicals. These productions, which
incorporated large choruses of beautiful women, were called "Coon
shows" in contrast to "Tom shows" and minstrel shows.[25] "Coon songs"

were simply ragtime songs with lyrics about Blacks, who were referred to as coons.[26]

Another landmark Black musical premiered during the 1898 season in New York. E. E. Rice had opened the summer season at the Casino Roof Garden (at 39th Street and Broadway), staging an entertainment (mostly vaudeville) entitled *Rice's Summer Nights*. On 5 July 1898, instead of the usual fare, the evening ended with an afterpiece named *Clorindy; or, The Origin of the Cakewalk*. This musical sketch, which had a cast of forty (later reduced to thirty), was produced by George W. Lederer and featured libretto and lyrics by Paul Laurence Dunbar and music by Will Marion Cook, a classically trained composer and conductor. *Clorindy*, starring Ernest Hogan, was the first musical to demonstrate what could be done with syncopated ragtime music. Also, *Clorindy* introduced the Cakewalk to the legitimate stage.[27] "The premiere," wrote Gerald Bordman, "marked the first time an all-Black effort played at a major house — albeit a roof garden — patronized exclusively by whites. The piece itself was so wildly successful it remained on the bill most of the summer."[28]

Cook recalled the performance of his cast: "My chorus sang like Russians, dancing meanwhile like Negroes, and cakewalking like angels, black angels! Negroes were at last on Broadway, and there to stay! Gone was the uff-dah of the minstrel! Gone the Massa Linkum stuff! We were artists and we were going a long, long way. . . . Nothing could stop us, and nothing did for a decade."[29]

Abbie Mitchell first appeared on the stage in 1898, at the age of fourteen, when she took over the lead in *Clorindy* during its run in Chicago.[30] Mitchell later became an actress in legitimate theatre.

It was in 1896 that the legendary comic team of Bert Williams and George Walker arrived in New York City singing one of the most popular tunes of the day, "Dora Dean." They had written the song as a tribute to the beauty of Dora Dean from *The Creole Show*. The chorus reads:

> Say, have you ever seen Miss Dora Dean,
> She is the finest gal you've ever seen,
> I'm a-goin' try and make this gal my queen
> Next Sunday mornin' I'm goin' marry Miss Dora Dean.[31]

In 1900 Williams and Walker starred in *Sons of Ham*, becoming the highest paid Black performers, a distinction they held throughout their careers.[32] Ada Walker, Lottie Williams, Abbie Mitchell, Anna E. Cook, Maggie Davis, Pauline Freeman, Clara Freeman, Estella Ware, Jennie

Sheppard, Odessa Warren, Fannie Winfred, Florence Elsworth, Lavina Jones, Nellie Wells, and Marie Williams were in the company.[33]

They had been touring with the show for two seasons before it opened on 3 March 1902 at the Grand Opera House in New York. Lottie Thompson (Williams), Hattie McIntosh, and Ada Walker (who changed her name to Aida) were in the cast.[34]

Sons of Ham concerned the efforts of Williams and Walker to masquerade as twins in a Colorado mining town in order to inherit a fortune. The masquerade proceeds well until it is learned that the real twins had mastered "acrobatics and gun-juggling" while at school. The fake twins spend much of their time trying to avoid display of these talents. The real twins arrive in the final act and Williams and Walker are forced to flee.[35]

Around 1902, when the show was playing at the Bijou Theatre in Washington, D.C., Florence Mills, the future star of *Shuffle Along* (1921) and *Blackbirds of 1926,* appeared in the production. Billed as "Baby Florence Mills, an Extra Added Attraction," she sang "Miss Hannah from Savannah." Mills, who was about eight years old, was taught the song by Ada Walker.[36]

Applauded for her dancing, Ada Walker was also known for her singing. Of all the hit songs she sang, she was most associated with "Miss Hannah from Savanah," from *Sons of Ham.* "This number," said Sampson, "was instrumental in making her one of the important figures in the Williams and Walker Company."[37] Her talents added much to the success of this organization. Van Vechten recalled that Ada "danced as few white women have danced."[38] Of this performer James Weldon Johnson commented: "Ada Overton Walker (Mrs. George Walker) was beyond comparison the brightest star among women on the Negro stage of the period; and it is a question whether or not she has since been surpassed. She was an attraction in the company not many degrees less than the two principals."[39]

One of the most popular forms of entertainment among White theatregoers was the operetta. In yet another attempt to break away from the stereotypical images of minstrelsy, Black composers and lyricists began developing Black operettas, hoping to appeal to White audiences. "Only then could black artists play the top theaters," said Helen Armstead-Johnson.[40] Black women gained prominence and stature with the development of operettas.

By 1902 Williams and Walker had produced an operetta called *In Dahomey.* The show, with music by Cook and lyrics by Dunbar, played at

THE QUEEN OF THE CAKEWALK
MISS AIDA OVERTON WALKER

1. Ada (Aida) Walker (c. 1906). Wife of comic George Walker and a star in her own right, she was an important figure in the Williams and Walker Company. Photo is gift to the author from Helen Johnson of The Armstead-Johnson Foundation for Theatre Research.

the New York Theatre in Times Square, the new center of the theatre district, making it the first Black show to open on Broadway itself.

> Despite the title, the new show spent little time in Africa. The first two acts concern Williams' and Walker's efforts to find a missing silver box. In the third act, the comic team escapes to Africa a step ahead of the law. They enjoy their new life in Africa and decide to remain where "Evah Dahkey Is a King." Of course, a few changes will have to be made if they remain, as Williams and Walker explain in their hit song "On Broadway in Dahomey."[41]

By the Spring of 1903 *In Dahomey* was in London, where it played at the Shaftesbury Theatre for seven months before touring the provinces.[42] While in London the company gave a command performance in the garden at Buckingham Palace for the birthday of the Prince of Wales.[43] This show not only established Williams and Walker's reputation, but it also established Black women as musical comedy stars. Hattie McIntosh, Lottie Williams (Mrs. Bert Williams), Ada Overton (Mrs. George Walker), and Abbie Mitchell (Mrs. Will Marion Cook) shared the lead with the comic duo. Inez Clough (who had remained in Europe entertaining for five years after the run of *Oriental America*), Ollie Burgoyne (also from *Oriental America*), Anita Bush, and Laura Bowman were in the chorus of *In Dahomey*. Bowman and Bush began their professional careers in *In Dahomey*, careers which were to span over forty years.

In Dahomey was a huge success, perhaps partly due to its novelty, according to Sandra Richards: "The mere fact that Negroes had assembled a cast of more than forty performers, written the book, composed the score, and stage managed a supposedly good musical comedy was in and of itself a novelty and worth the trip to the theatre."[44]

Around 1904 Ollie (Olga) Burgoyne traveled to St. Petersburg, Russia, where she opened a lingerie shop and used Black models in the window. In addition to being a businesswoman, Burgoyne headed a company of fourteen players. When the Revolution occurred, she and her troupe were vacationing in Austria. Unable to return to Russia, Burgoyne came back to the United States with little money and few belongings.[45] "Miss Burgoyne's specialty was dancing," said Sampson, "and her forte was the Brazilian dance, the Snake dance and the famous Spanish dance."[46] Producing, choreographing, and performing in musicals throughout the 1920s, Ollie Burgoyne toured Europe at least fifteen times with various acts during her career, playing in Egypt, Turkey, Germany, Denmark, Sweden, France, Hungary, and Switzerland.[47] Burgoyne was last seen on the stage as one of the three witches in the Federal Theatre Project's all-Black *Macbeth* at the Lafayette Theatre in 1936.

In 1904 Will Marion Cook's *The Southerners,* a musical of life on the plantation, was presented at the New York Theatre. Laura Bowman appeared in the chorus.[48] Abbie Mitchell portrayed Mandy Lou, a principal, and Ida Forsyne danced a solo.[49]

The Southerners has the distinction of being "Broadway's first interracial musical." Because of this, there were fears that the show would cause trouble. The reviewer for the *New York Times* described the tension of opening night:

> When the chorus of real live coons walked in for the cake (walk) last night at the New York Theatre, mingling with the white members of the cast, there were those in the audience who trembled in their seats, as if expecting an . . . explosion. . . . But it presently became evident that the spirit of harmony reigned. The magician was discovered on inquiry to be the Negro composer Will Marion Cook, who all alone had succeeded in harmonizing the racial broth as skillfully as he had harmonized the accompanying score.[50]

Williams and Walker's next hit operetta, *Abyssinia,* with book by Jessie Shipp and music by Cook, opened on 20 February 1906 at the Majestic Theatre, then located at Columbus Circle on the corner of West 58th Street. In addition to a cast of over twenty chorus girls, several women played principal parts with the two stars. They included Lottie Williams, Ada Overton Walker, Hattie McIntosh, Annie Ross, and Maggie Davis.[51] During the run of the show, Anita Bush appeared in the chorus.[52]

In 1901 Bob Cole teamed with J. Rosamond Johnson, brother of James Weldon Johnson and a popular musician and singer who arranged many well-known Negro spirituals. Later, in 1906, Cole and the Johnson brothers composed *The Shoo-Fly Regiment.* This operetta, starring Cole and J. Rosamond Johnson, opened on 6 August 1907 at the Bijou Theatre in New York. The featured women performers included Nettie Glenn, Elizabeth Williams, Mamie Butler, Mollie Dill, and Fannie Wise.[53] During the run of the show, Inez Clough left *Shoo-Fly* to join Williams and Walker in *Abyssinia.* She stayed with the company until it disbanded in 1910.[54]

Williams and Walker appeared together for the last time in their most praised production, *Bandana* (or *Bandanna) Land.* This show, with musical numbers staged by Ada Walker and music composed by Cook and Will Vodery with lyricist Alex Rodgers, opened on 3 Febru-

ary 1908 at the Majestic Theatre in Brooklyn, New York. During the
run of the show, George, suffering from paresis, became too ill to perform. In February 1909, one year after the opening of *Bandana Land,*
Walker was forced to retire from the stage. Before the show was revised
due to Walker's absence, Ada imitated her husband performing his
theme song, "Bon Bon Buddy."[55] "Cartoons of Ada appeared in the
newspapers showing her in a straw hat, plaid four-botton suit and
spats, carrying white gloves and a cane, her boufant long hair swept
under her hat, dressed for her impersonation of the 'Bon Bon
Buddy.' "[56] Abbie Mitchell, one of the principals in the show, sang "Red
Red Rose."[57]

In 1909 Abbie Mitchell starred as the lead soprano, Minnehaha (singing "Cupid Is an Indian Pickininny"), in Cole and J. Rosamond Johnson's operetta *The Red Moon.* The show, which opened on 3 May 1909
in New York at the Majestic Theatre, toured England, where Abbie
sang a command performance for Czar Nicholas II of Russia.[58] Blanche
Deas, who was later to perform in a production that made theatrical
history, appeared in the chorus.[59]

The storyline of *Red Moon* combined the folklore of Blacks and Indi-
ans:

> The red moon of the title was an omen of bad luck to the blacks in
> the cast and a call to war for the Indians. Needless to say, this
> dual meaning led to several plot complications. Minnehaha, half-
> Indian and half-black, lives with her mother on a Virginia farm.
> Her delinquent father, Chief Lowdog, decides that he misses his
> long-lost daughter, so he kidnaps her to his reservation. Slim
> Brown (Cole) and Plunk Green (Johnson) try to rescue the chief's
> daughter from her father's clutches. Brown and Green disguise
> themselves as Indians and depart for the West. After several In-
> dian war dances in the second act, Plunk rescues Minnehaha, and
> the chief and his wife are reconciled.[60]

A few months after the closing of *Bandana Land,* Bert Williams decided to produce and star in *Mr. Lode of Koal* (1909). A full-length production in the Williams and Walker tradition, *Mr. Lode of Koal*
featured many of the performers from previous Williams and Walker
shows. Ada Walker, however, refused to sign on. Although she had been
offered a contract, "she and the management have not been able to
agree on several items," reported the *New York Age.*[61]

After Walker took over the lead in *Red Moon,* Williams signed Lottie
Grady, a showgirl from the Pekin Theatre in Chicago, to co-star with
him. Unlike other Williams and Walker efforts, this show did not re-

ceive the support of the press or the public. *Mr. Lode of Koal,* which
opened on 1 November 1909 at the Majestic Theatre, was Williams's
last performance in an all-Black show.[62] In addition to Lottie Grady,
who played Mysteria, there were ten principal female parts. Inez
Clough appeared in the chorus as a flower girl.[63] Like Clough and
Blanche Deas (from *Red Moon*), Lottie Grady also figured in a later
event that made theatrical history.

On 8 May 1911 the Smart Set, a Black producing/acting company,
opened with *His Honor the Barber* at the Majestic Theatre for eight
performances. This musical "features the dreams of a barber named
Raspberry Snow. Snow wishes to shave the president of the United
States and elope with the beautiful Lily White. His wishes come true in
Act II, but it is only a dream sequence. Snow awakes to the disappoint-
ment in Act III."[64] The reviewer for the *New York Dramatic Mirror*
wrote:

> S. H. Dudley and Aida Overton Walker lead the contingent with
> much assurance and allow no dull moments while they hold the
> stage. Dudley is a quiet comedian of much resourcefulness, while
> Miss Walker, as is well known, is the best Negro comedienne to-
> day. Her tomboy number, her Spanish song and dance, and her
> impersonation of a Negro "chappie," the last of which is the real
> hit of the play, are minutely favorable characterizations. With
> such material as Dudley and Miss Walker have, they do won-
> ders.[65]

From 1911 to 1912 "Aida Walker and her Abyssinia Girls" were
vaudeville favorites. During the period 1912–1914, instead of performing, she produced and managed acts such as the "Happy Girls" and the
"Porto Rico Girls." The last production with which she was associated
was given on 16 August 1914 at the Manhattan Casino. A few months
later, on 11 October 1914, at the age of thirty-four, she died.[66]

In 1912 the Smart Set returned to New York with *Mr. Beans from
Boston,* starring Sherman H. Dudley. They played at Hurtig and
Seamon's Music Hall for a short run.[67] After the closing of *Mr. Beans
from Boston,* Black productions on the professional stage ended for five
seasons. In 1910 Bert Williams signed with the *Ziegfeld Follies* and
stayed with the annual editions of the show until 1920. Soon after
Walker's death in 1911, Bob Cole's health faltered; he retired from the
stage and died, also in 1911. By this time, Ernest Hogan had also died.
The importance of the leadership of these men was so great that their
departure left no producer/director/writer/composer teams to develop
Black musical comedy for Broadway. So, from 1912 to 1917, except for
Bert Williams, Blacks did not perform on the Broadway stage.

During these years, however, there was an aggressive effort by Black artists and others to establish a theatre in the Black community. This venture produced in 1915 Harlem's first community theatre company, the Lafayette Players. The Lafayette Players were well received, presenting much of what was being produced on Broadway. The company is reported to have given creditable performances of melodramas such as *The Count of Monte Cristo, Dr. Jekyll and Mr. Hyde, Madame X, The Servant in the House, The Thirteenth Chair,* and other plays of that caliber, as well as musical comedy shows.[68]

Abbie Mitchell, for a long time the company's most praised leading lady, revealed the importance of the pioneering efforts of these performers and the reason why they presented such plays:

> The men and women of the Negro group who have paved the way for all Negroes in the theatres in the United States in acting came from a small group known as the Lafayette Theatre . . . it wasn't possible to see a Negro acting a serious part, small or large, on Broadway. White men and women were "browned down" to play the roles. The reason for this, as expressed by the producers, was that we, the Negroes, hadn't any deep emotions. Well, the old Lafayette Players proved we not only had deep emotions, but could project them to trained and un-trained audiences. At that time, thirty-two years ago, there weren't any serious dramas written by our own, hence we were compelled to play Broadway success. . . . "Broadwayites," producers and managers came to ridicule, but remained to applaud. From then on they began to tryout individuals downtown; the ice was broken, doors were opened. Perhaps someday some one of our poets will dig deep into the well of our folklore unashamedly and bring forth some play about our men and women of whom we can be proud. . . .[69]

The success of the Lafayette Theatre prompted the founding of stock companies at the Lincoln Theatre, also in Harlem, and Black theatres in other major cities. (the Lafayette Players at the Dunbar Theatre in Philadelphia and Lafayette Players at the Howard Theatre in Washington, D.C.).[70]

Black women played an active role, both as entertainers and businesswomen, in the development of the Lafayette stock acting company. Some of the women who performed in this troupe had been a part of the Isham, Black Patti, Cole and Johnson, and Williams and Walker companies: Laura Bowman, Mattie Wikes, Marie Young, Abbie Mitchell, Lottie Grady, Inez Clough, Elizabeth Williams, and Anita Bush. Black theatre scholars credit Bush with galvanizing these performers into action. Besides conceiving the idea of organizing the group, Bush brought the first permanent company to the Lafayette Theatre.

During the period that Blacks did not perform in mainstream professional theatre in New York, vital changes took place: Black artists in New York who had for decades played to predominantly white audiences were now playing to a predominantly Black audience, and the freedom from the taboos and restrictions of forty years gave them an opportunity to perform in offerings ranging from crude burlesque to Broadway drama.[71] This move from Broadway to Harlem, like minstrelsy, provided another training period for Black performers to sharpen their acting skills; soon they would be thrust onto the professional stage once again.

"April 5, 1917 is the date of the most important single event in the entire history of the Negro in the American theatre," wrote James Weldon Johnson, "for it marks the beginning of a new era."[72] On this day, three *dramatic* plays were presented by the Colored Players at the Garden Theatre (formerly Wallack's) in Madison Square Garden in New York City. These plays, collectively entitled *Three Plays for a Negro Theatre*, were written by Ridgley Torrence, produced by Mrs. Emily Hapgood, and directed and designed by Robert Edmond Jones. The author, producer, and director/designer were White. The first play of the evening was *The Rider of Dreams*, a folk comedy; followed by *Granny Maumee*, a folk tragedy; and ending with *Simon the Cyrenian*, "A Passion Interlude."

Granny Maumee had an all-female cast with Marie Jackson-Stuart playing the title role, Fannie Tarkington as Pearl, and Blanche Deas (from *Red Moon*) as Sapphie. This piece depicts a Black woman of royal African ancestry who despises Whites because they had wrongly accused her son of murder and burned him in a fire that blinded her when she tried to save him. When her granddaughter returns home with a mulatto child, Granny Maumee tries to place a voodoo curse upon the White father, but she has lost her powers because she has been a Christian for a long time. *The Rider of Dreams* presents Lucy Sparrow (played by Blanche Deas), a hardworking rural woman who has saved enough money from her meager earnings to buy her dream, a home. Her husband, Madison Sparrow, a dreamer who spends most of his time daydreaming, steals the money. In turn, he is robbed but manages to get the money back and continues to "ride his dreams." *Simon the Cyrenian* is about the Black man, Simon, who was forced to carry Christ's cross to Mt. Calvary.[73] Inez Clough (from *Oriental America* and *Shoo-Fly Regiment*, the Williams and Walker Company, and the Lafayette Players) portrayed Procula, the wife of Pilate, and Lottie Grady (from *Mr. Lode of Koal* and the Pekin and Lafayette Theatres) played Acte, Princess of Egypt.

In addition to integrating Blacks into the audience, the presentation of this landmark production helped to refute the generally held belief that while Black performers were natural singers and dancers, they did not possess the ability to portray dramatic characters. Displaying a wide range of acting skills, these players received almost unanimous praise from the critics, the press, and the public. According to the critic for the New York *Globe*, "These Negroes play Negro plays. They reveal the soul of the people. They are not propagandizing. They do not demand, argue, or protest. They are really artists."[74] The reviewer for the *New Republic* reported, "It is, all things considered, as fine an enterprise as the American theatre has seen for years. . . . The actors had unusual power and charm."[75] The critic for the *New York Dramatic Mirror* wrote:

> To Mrs. Emily Hapgood, then, belongs, the credit for a significant experiment – that of testing the possibilities of negro drama interpreted by colored actors before cosmopolitan audiences. . . . More completely trained white actor could not have felt nor made others feel the spirit of "The Rider of Dreams." . . . Mrs. Hapgood's negro players are one of the big events of the season and deserve every possible encouragement.[76]

The *New York Age* began its review, "Negro Actors Make Debut In Drama at Garden Theatre; Given Most Cordial Welcome," written by Lester A. Walton, on the front page. According to Walton (who would eventually become manager of the Lafayette Theatre): "Judging from the most cordial reception accorded the ambitious Thespians, who were compelled to respond to encore after encore at the end of each playlet, the launching of this bold dramatic endeavor was an unqualified success."[77]

On the other hand, all of the press was not favorable to *Three Plays*. Burns Mantle claimed that the acting was "bad": "The Negro is not racially adapted to the expression of tragedy or serious emotion, usually displaying an imitative and stilted style and a grotesque rather than a genuine sense of feeling." He added: "We feel it would be better for him to be away from Broadway influences."[78]

In an article published in the *New York Post,* James Weldon Johnson provided some insight as to the reasons why Mantle would express such racist views:

> The Negro has long had a place on the American stage; and the race has produced a long line of well known minstrels, comedians, and dancers. . . . But the Negro's place on the American stage has largely been limited and circumscribed. The idea that the colored

performer could do anything else besides making an audience laugh seems rarely to have entered a manager's head. This attitude on the part of managers has been due largely to the popular national conception of the Negro as a happy-go-lucky, laughing, shuffling, banjo-picking being; a conception which ignores the other side of the truth—that the life of every thinking Negro in the United States is a part of a great tragedy.[79]

Torrence avoided stereotypes in the portrayal of his Black characters. Instead, they were realistic and sympathetic. Through his plays Torrence helped to advance the development of Black Drama, the Black character, and the Black artist. He explained his reasons for writing them:

> It was not only the capacity of the Negro as an actor that I wished to exploit. It was also the extraordinary dramatic richness of his daily life. The Negro has been a race apart and usually a race in subjection. . . . [The Negro race's] life under slavery with its intense but seemingly helpless longing for liberty produced in it a certain epic spirit, unconscious of course. . . . In modern life, the Negro comes face to face with many tragedies unknown to the Anglo-Saxon.[80]

After playing at the Garden for eighteen performances, *Three Plays for a Negro Theatre* moved to the Garrick Theatre on 16 April where it ran for one week. On 6 April 1917, the day after the opening, the United States declared war against Germany. Even though *Three Plays* was a critical success, the increasing tension of World War I became too much for this show, as well as for some stronger shows; on 23 April 1917 it closed.[81]

The pioneering efforts of Black artists during this period to break away from traditional "darky shows" were significant. Refining and capitalizing on ideas first established by the Hyers Sisters, the theatricals presented were novel in plot, dancing, and music, introducing to a wider audience African settings and themes, urbanized, upwardly mobile Blacks, and love interests. All of these innovations provided opportunities for Black performers to enlarge the "horizons of acceptable black characterizations." "Gone are the days of the happy life on the plantation with dear ole Massa;" wrote Sandra Richards. "Instead Negroes strut, wear modish clothes and impressive jewelry, as did Walker in sporting a breast sash of diamonds in *In Dahomey*."[82] And now that song lyrics were bold and sassy (like those in *Sons of Ham*), Ada Walker could sing

> I want to be the leading lady,
> I want to play the real star part, . . .
> I'll make Bernhardt look like thirty cents. . . .[83]

These productions represented the transitional period between minstrelsy and the Black musical comedy and the "New Negro" of the 1920s.[84]

The emergence and development of Black musicals of this era "is of great importance to the history of American musical theatre." These shows were forerunners of the coming Broadway musical. In addition to the traditional types of music that audiences expected, these Black musicals moved ragtime songs and Black dancing "from their accustomed place in vaudeville and made them" acceptable as an integral part "of the developing American musical comedy."[85]

The talents of so many Black artists during this period helped to establish a form that was not imported from Europe or the English stage, but was indigenous to the United States.[86] These productions added a new dimension to American theatre entertainment, laying a foundation for public acceptance of images of Black men and women on the stage in other than "burlesque" roles. Through them, the Black artist-performer left his distinctive mark upon the development of American musical comedy. As James V. Hatch put it, without the contributions of these artists the "American musical might still be waltzing with an umpah-pah-pah to the descendants of *Merry Widow* and *Naughty Marietta.*"[87]

At the time, some Black men had received recognition as singers, dancers, and comedians in minstrelsy and in "specialty acts." Several of these men married, teaming with their wives and creating vaudeville acts. Sam Lucas and his wife Carrie, known as "Mr. and Mrs. Sam Lucas," were a featured act in *The Creole Show.* Laura Bowman and Pete Hampton formed "Hampton and Bowman" and performed throughout the world. "Johnson and Dean" was still another husband/wife team. Lottie Williams and Ada Walker, the wives of Bert Williams and George Walker, respectively, performed principal roles in the landmark Williams and Walker productions. Will Marion Cook wrote several very popular songs for his wife, Abbie Mitchell. These turn-of-the-century Black male entertainers were both teachers and promoters of Black female entertainers, providing them with performing opportunities.

3

THE CLASS ACTS: THREE BLACK
FEMALE SINGERS AND DANCERS

At the turn of the century, Black entertainers were redefining and refining their image on the American stage. By this time, both individual and team acts had developed the sophistication and elegance of their White counterparts. According to Marshall and Jean Stearns, these "class acts," "among other things, were an expression of the Negroes' drive toward equality and respectability."[1] These writers point out that "the pioneering team Johnson and Dean was perhaps the first to break ground for the class acts."[2] By 1900 Dora Dean, dubbed the "Black Venus," had gained international fame. Born in Indianapolis (but considering Minneapolis her home) Dora Dean Babbige and her husband Charles Johnson, one of the end men from *The Creole Show,* were cakewalkers who headlined here and abroad. They first met while playing in *The Creole Show* and then decided to form a team. After learning new routines, they left the show for vaudeville, and were soon successful.[3]

Creative and innovative, their dancing established several firsts. In 1891 they introduced the cakewalk at Hammerstein's Roof Garden in New York City. They were also the first dance team in vaudeville, Black or White, in 1901 to wear evening clothes on stage, at Koster and Bial's, also in New York City. In 1897 Johnson and Dean became the first Black dance team to play on Broadway.[4] In addition to being talented, Johnson and Dean were a handsome couple. The 8 April 1901 issue of the New York *Telegraph* called them "the best dressed team in vaudeville."[5] Dean, a fair-complexioned, beautiful woman with a plump, hourglass figure, was "the first Negro Woman to wear a thousand-dollar costume on stage."[6] "At the height of their success," said Sampson, "many of Dora's gowns cost more than $1000 each and were copied by Lillian Russell, Sarah Bernhardt and other big names on Broadway."[7] *Variety* noted:

> ... "Miss Dean and Her Fantoms," the act is called. It is colored and the classiest of its kind. Miss Dean for her entrance gown chose a pink satin dress with a crystalled tunic of old blue. A large black hat with airgrettes was worn. A second change was a harem costume. The bloomers were pale blue and the dress purple chiffon. The last gown was artistic in coloring as well as model. A foundation of salmon pink satin was covered in white net, edged in white fox.[8]

Johnson and Dean were so popular and exceptional that in 1908 they were signed by the prestigious William Morris Agency.[9] They made the cakewalk famous playing winter gardens in Budapest, Berlin, Hungary, and Vienna.[10] "On tours abroad, according to dancers in the company, she had the crowned heads of Europe literally at her feet."[11] While the team was in Germany, artist Ernest von Heilmann was so inspired by her beauty that he bought Dora Dean's theatrical contract so she could pose for him. The picture was exhibited throughout America after it was unveiled at the coronation of King Edward in London in 1902.[12] A cigarette company printed her picture on a card as "The Sweet Caporal Girl" and enclosed it in packs of cigarettes.[13] A popular song of the day, written by Williams and Walker as a tribute to her beauty, asked, "Have you met Miss Dora Dean, prettiest girl you've ever seen?"

Married in 1893, the couple separated at the start of World War I.[14] Both Johnson and Dean formed acts of their own and continued to work. A *Variety* review of her show at the American Roof Garden Theatre in New York City, dated 26 June 1914, read:

> At last a "Pick act" without a white woman for the feature. With three girls and as many boys, Dora Dean and Co. make a fast going aggregation. . . . The boys' dancing at the finish leaves a fine impression. The act is dressed well, the girls making a number of changes, while the boys look very nifty in dark trousers and later in evening dress. The act should go very well on the big small time.[15]

Prompted by the popularity of her own company, Dora Dean organized several successful all-Black singing/dancing troupes that appeared in Germany, Russia, England, and France.[16]

2. Dora Dean (1905), "The Black Venus." The song "Dora Dean" (1896) was written and popularized by Bert Williams and George Walker as a tribute to her beauty. Teamed with her husband, Charles Johnson, she was a cakewalker here and abroad. Photo courtesy of Hatch-Billops Collection.

Dora Dean left show business for a while and became partners with Mattie Wilkes (from *The Octoroons* and *Oriental America*) in a lingerie and hat shop in New York City. Wilkes who had been performing in Russia, had returned to New York when World War I erupted. Previously she had owned a lingerie and hat shop there.[17]

In 1934 Dora Dean traveled to Hollywood to do *Georgia Rose,* an all-Black film. While there, she and Charles Johnson decided to revive their old act.[18] In 1936, although both were over fifty, they staged a "comeback" at Connie's Inn in New York, then appeared briefly in nightclubs throughout the country.[19] By this time, however, motion pictures were replacing vaudeville and their act was shortlived. Johnson and Dean returned to Minneapolis where Dora Dean died on 13 December 1949.[20] "Acclaimed as 'the originators of high-class Negro show business,' Johnson and Dean established the roles of the genteel Negro couple on the American stage – the courtly gentleman and the gracious lady."[21] She did not, however, become an actress in legitimate theatre.

Another very early pivotal female figure who did become an actress on the musical stage was Madame M. Sissieretta Jones, better known as "Black Patti." A trained concert singer, Madame Jones pioneered with her own company. Of the other competing Black roadshows touring the country, hers was the most prestigious.[22] Born Matilda Joyner on 5 January 1869, in Portsmouth, Virginia, the daughter of Reverend Jeremiah M. and Henrietta B. Joyner (a soprano of exceptional talent), she and her family migrated to Providence, Rhode Island, in 1876. Sissy, as she was called as a child, began to attract local attention singing in the Pond Street Baptist Church Sunday School entertainments. At fifteen, she started studying at the Providence Academy of Music. She continued her classical training at the New England Conservatory of Music in Boston.[23]

She made her professional debut in New York City in 1888 at Wallack's Theatre, "a place where no other colored singer had been privileged to shine," announced a press release.[24] The next day, the *New York Clipper* dubbed her "The Black Patti" after Adelina Patti, the reigning White opera singer of the day. The paper said, "She sings like Patti without the slightest effort."[25] Although she appreciated the compliment, Madame Jones disliked the comparison. In an interview some years later, she said: " 'But I do not begin to sing like Patti can. I have been anxious to drop the name but it had been so identified with me, it is now impossible.' "[26] According to Dr. Carl R. Gross, "her voice in its early stages was a decided contralto and as it matured, still contained the velvety richness so noticeable in such singers as Scalchi and others."[27]

On 4 September 1883 she married David Richard Jones. Dick Jones, a one-eyed impresario who managed some of her business affairs, had definite plans for his wife's career. Because Mme. Jones "was very dark skinned, with Negroid features, he took her to London in 1890 to begin arsenic 'treatment' which was supposed to lighten her coloring and straighten her hair."[28] As later photographs attest, the "treatment" did not work. Sissieretta Jones and her husband had one child, who died. In 1898 she divorced Jones, a racetrack and gambling man, because he mismanaged her money. However, she kept the name Madame Sissieretta Jones for the stage.[29]

By 1891 she had toured the West Indies and South America with the Tennessee Jubilee Singers for six months.[30] Black Patti received wide recognition after she had performed with Jules Levy and his famous Band at Madison Square Garden on 26–28 April 1892 at a Jubilee Spectacle and Cakewalk. After singing before 75,000 people in one week, she remarked, "'I woke up famous after singing at the Garden and didn't know it.' "[31] Two nights later, she sang for a large audience at the Academy of Music in Brooklyn. Such was her success that rumors that the managers of the Metropolitan Opera House had signed her to sing the dark roles in *Aida* and *L'Africaine* began circulating.[32] Although racial prejudice prevented her from appearing there at the time, she helped lay the foundation for Marian Anderson and others who followed.

Black Patti went on to develop a large following singing on the concert stage. Earning more than $100 a day, she sang at the World's Fair in Toronto, Canada 1892, and before 7,500 people in two nights at Saratoga's Congress Spring Park 1892.[33] In September 1892 she sang for President Benjamin Harrison at the White House, and later for President Grover Cleveland.[34] She also sang for Presidents Theodore Roosevelt and William McKinley.[35]

Sissieretta Jones was managed by the American Lecture and Musical Agency. Owned by Major James B. Pond, the agency handled such celebrities as Mark Twain, Henry Ward Beecher, and Sir Edwin Arnold.[36] In 1893 Major Pond demanded and received $2000 (the highest salary ever paid to a Black artist) for her one-week engagement at the Pittsburgh Exposition. On 22 February 1893 she sang before 7,000 at the Talmage Tabernacle in Brooklyn, New York. She performed before 300,000 at the Buffalo Exposition, and 12,000 in Congress Hall Park at the Chicago World's Fair.[37] Mrs. Alberta Wilson, who was also under contract to Major Pond, accompanied Madame Jones. "At a concert in Louisville, Ky., to the people who had never seen a finished colored pianist, she was curiosity and revelation."[38]

Appearing before such large audiences had its drawbacks: Because of low admission fees that encouraged attendance by the "popular" audi-

3. Sissieretta Jones (Classical Singer). From 1896 to 1915, she headed "Black Patti's Troubadours," one of the first important Black musical organizations to tour the North, South, and Canada successfully. Photo courtesy of Carl R. Gross Papers, Box 41-1, Folder 11, Moorland-Spingarn Research Center, Howard University.

ence, Madame Jones, like the Hyers Sisters before her (who, in order to earn a living, performed in minstrel shows), performed a repertory that would appeal to public tastes. She sang "plantation pieces" like "Swanee River," and favorites such as "Comin' Thro' the Rye" and "Maggie the Cows are in the Clover." The *Pittsburgh Press* noted: " 'Black Patti' has a sweet, well modulated voice and yet it is powerful enough to be heard throughout the main building. She had considerable to contend with, too, in her afternoon performance in the noise and confusion created by over 3,500 school children, who despite the efforts of teachers and policemen could not keep still."[39]

Unlike her White contemporaries Lillian Nordica and Emma Emaes, Sissieretta Jones could not aspire to a career on the legitimate American operatic stage, especially the Metropolitan Opera House.[40] She was painfully aware of the restrictions imposed upon her by color. An excerpt from an interview in the *Detroit Tribune* revealed: "Her [Mrs. Jones] favorite songs are from the opera 'L'Africaine.' She would like very much to sing in that opera, but she pathetically said: 'They tell me my color is against me.' "[41] Whenever Madame Jones encountered racism and was asked by the press about her experiences, she would speak out. According to an undated article, when questioned by a reporter for the Louisville *Commercial* concerning how she felt about her performance before a segregated house in Louisville, Kentucky, she replied: " 'It's so strange; I never have met with anything like it before.' " When the reporter responded, " 'What do you mean?' " she answered: " 'Why, putting the colored people off in the gallery and leaving all those vacant seats downstairs. Why the house would have been crowded if "they" had allowed them to have seats downstairs. I felt very much disappointed: I have never before had such an experience, and I could not help feeling it. . . . I think people of my own race ought not to be shut out in this way.' "[42]

On 13 February 1892 Jones achieved the distinction of becoming the "first Black artist to present a concert at Carnegie Hall."[43] Afterward Morris Reno, president of the Carnegie Music Hall Association of New York, engaged Black Patti for a tour of the United States and Europe. She performed in Europe successfully for almost an entire year, premiering first in Berlin. The *Berliner Zeitung* reported: "no sooner had the real Patti departed than a most worthy substitute appeared in the person of Black Patti from America."[44] She sang in St. Petersburg, Munich, Milan, Cologne, and Paris. In London she gave a command performance for King Edward and for the Prince of Wales.[45]

During the Nineties, the "Star System"—the star rather than the play—dominated the stage. Touring operatic companies had become popular. Realizing that her operatic career was limited, however, Ma-

dame Jones embarked on a theatrical career.[46] Upon her return from
her second European tour, her new managers (Rudolph Voelckel and J.
Nolan of New York) hired Bob Cole (who had been a comedian in *The
Creole Show*) to write and stage an all-Black show for Mme. Jones, a
show that could compete with *Oriental America*. In 1896 "Black Patti's
Troubadours" opened at Proctor's 58th Street Theatre in New York.[47]
Sampson credited *The Troubadours* with being the "first successful
black road show to tour the East and South."[48] In pattern, this production was similar to minstrelsy. "The first part was a sketchy farce interspersed with songs and choruses and ending with a buck-dance
contest. Then followed the olio. The finale was termed: 'The Operatic
Kaleidoscope,' and in it 'Black Patti' appeared in songs and operatic selections with the chorus."[49]

Although this was bold for a Black woman at the time, Mme. Jones's
activity in the show was not truly groundbreaking. As Errol Hill observed, "long before the Oriental America Company or the Black Patti
Troubadours of the 1890s, the Hyers sisters introduced the singing of
operatic selections to round out a performance."[50]

Black Patti's Troubadours were widely accepted. According to a review in the *Indianapolis Freeman:*

> Vaudeville, comedy, burlesque, and opera interpreted by fifty of
> the best artists ever organized for this style of entertainment will
> be the stage offering of "Black Patti's Troubadours" on the occa-
> sion of their performance in this city. The company is practically a
> double one with "Black Patti" as the star of the operatic and sing-
> ing forces. . . . She sustains the principal roles of "The Grand
> Duchess," "Carmen," "Bohemian Girl," "Trovatore," "Lucia," "Mari-
> tana," "Tartar," and "The Daughter of the Regiment." . . . The work
> of Black Patti and the company has received the highest marks of
> public approval and the forthcoming performances here will
> doubtless be highly appreciated.[51]

The original "Troubadours" cast included Stella Wiley and Bob Cole
in the comedy sketches; May Bobee, the Creole nightingale; and thirty
chorus girls. Maggie Davis, Ada Overton (Walker), Lena Wise, the De-
Wolf Sisters, and Madame Reed were in the company.[52]

The Troubadours played a grueling forty-five-week season from July
to May, traveling thousands of miles yearly, appearing in every city and
town with available theatre space.[53] "Madam Jones enjoys the distinction of appearing in more consecutive performances than any other living singer of her time."[54] According to the Stearns, "Black Patti herself
came close to beating the white concert-singers at their own game."[55]

In addition to the show written by Cole, Black Patti toured in other productions, including *At Jolly Coon-ey Island* (1898). A skit starring Ernest Hogan, *At Jolly Coon-ey Island* was "based on a minstrel format with spontaneous buffoonery interspersed with song."[56] The following season the Troubadours presented *A Rag-time Frolic at Ras-bury Park.* "Exaggerated comedy, plenty of character work, lightening dancing by both men and women, comic songs and acrobatic fun are chief ingredients of the skit," said the *Detroit Free Press.*[57]

Around 1900, in a step toward linking the separate parts of a "variety show" into a unified musical comedy with a beginning, middle, and end, the Troubadours added comedy sketches with a slight plot.[58] About their first one-act farce, the *Evening Mail* (St. John, New Brunswick) commented: "The programme [Troubadours] began with a very funny ragtime comedy skit called 'A Darktown Frolic on the Rialto.' There was not great depth of plot to this jolly absurdity but the action was spirited and the specialties were of the very best and immensely pleasing."[59]

Capitalizing on Williams and Walker's *In Dahomey,* the Troubadours presented *Dooney Dreamland* in 1903. The *Augusta Chronicle* described *Dooney Dreamland* as an "up-to-date comedy with its operatic kaleidoscope containing a group of plantation pastimes and an 'Offenbach review.' "[60] The new show for 1908 was *The Blackville Strollers.* This skit included comedians "Tutt" Whitney and Slim Henderson, Gus Hall, Sarah Green, the Troubadour Quartet (a group of female singers), and tenor George Day.[61]

By 1910, as productions became more structured, Black Patti had integrated her operatic singing into the plot of the sketches.[62] The 11 March 1911 *Columbia Dispatch* (Ohio) noted the change with the three-act *A Trip to Africa* (1910): "Miss Jones, in gorgeous raiment, steps forth in the jungles of Africa among the half-breeds and is acclaimed the princess."[63] This role made Mme. Jones "part of the action and hence brought about a consolidation of the serious and the humorous into the one unified form."[64] A musical farce, *A Trip to Africa* concerns a college professor who steals money and goes to Africa to rescue a missionary being held there for ransom.[65]

During the Fall of 1911, the Troubadours opened with a three-act play entitled *In the Jungles.* The *Louisville Post* gave this description of the plot: "A relief party has been sent to the jungle to effect the release of Cynthia Brown, a school teacher, who has been lost in the wilds."[66] In the last act of *In the Jungles* Mme. Jones "assumes the part of the sister of the head of the Baptist seminary."[67] In the same piece, "Sissieretta Jones appears in the role of Queen Le-Ku-Li, queen of the Gumbula Tribe."[68]

During the 1912 season the Troubadours opened with *Captain Jackson,* a three-act piece featuring Black Patti and Harrison Stewart. The *Fort Worth Star-Telegram* provided the following description: "Captain Jasper, as presented by the Black Patti company is not a minstrel show. It's a musical comedy about government papers stolen by a renegade officer of Negro troops to be sold to Cheteka, queen of a Philippine tribe, and the efforts to apprehend him."[69]

Sometime later, the name of Mme. Jones's company was changed to "Black Patti Musical Company." As her show began to resemble the musical comedy format with a storyline, she performed small speaking roles but remained the featured singer.[70]

During the 1914–1915 season, the Troubadours added *Lucky Sam* to their repertory. In it, "Sissieretta Jones becomes a part of the cast of the play, her musical repertory originating out of the dramatic situation,"[71] eliminating the need for the "Operatic Kaleidoscope" altogether.

Although she attempted to keep her personal life private, her public appearances were grandly staged. In 1900 she "married" Rudolph Voelckel, her Jewish manager.

> They traveled together for fifteen years in what was advertised as a $30,000 private railroad car fitted with gold plush upholstery and hand-carved pianos. Eubie Blake, the Negro showman who joined the troupe as a youngster, serving as Madame Jones' private errand boy with regular orders to run to grocery stores for a nickel's worth of her favorite ginger snaps, remembered that Voelckel insisted that a red carpet had to be laid on the sidewalk from the stage door to the hack every time she came to and from the theater.[72]

As a boy, Eubie Blake had lived near Sissieretta Jones in Baltimore. " 'I never heard anybody with a voice like hers,' " recalled Blake, " 'and I heard the original white Patti, too – when she sang 'The Prison Song,' first in the original key and then an octave higher, it was like she had a wonderful bird in her throat. She had a range like Yma Sumac and a fine operatic voice.' "[73] Some years later, Mme. Jones's exceptional talents and sophisticated manner were still beyond reproach. An unidentified, undated article remarked: " 'Black Patti' still retains that charm of voice and manner which won her an international reputation as a singer years ago. If nature had been more kind to her in the matter of complexion, she could have been at this time the pet prima donna of society. As it is, she is one of the highest salaried singers on the stage and is recognized as an artist of extraordinary vocal ability."[74]

Although Madame Jones enjoyed the status of being one of the most respected Black celebrities of the day, she still encountered racial contempt.

> She was engaged to sing at the Madison Street Presbyterian Church in Baltimore, the gospel cafeteria of the first families. Arriving in the afternoon for a private rehearsal, her voice drifted across the street to the ears of one of the dowagers who was entertaining her club. Whose voice is that? On being told it was the voice of Black Patti, she said, I'll allow her to sing for our party. She dispatched her colored cook to invite her over. Madame Jones looked at the cook, saying tell your mistress if she will contact my managers, arrange for an engagement, I will be happy to sing for her, but it will be several months. The cook returned and were the faces of the blue bloods red.[75]

The exact date of Mme. Jones's last appearance is not established, but in 1916 she left the stage to care for her mother. There had been speculations that she would return. Instead, she retired to her nine-room home at 7 Wheaton Street in Providence, Rhode Island. Soon after, she joined the Congdon Street Baptist Church and lived quietly with some of her treasures of former days.[76]

Madame Jones, a woman of unusual generosity, took care of homeless children until she was penniless. Forced to sell her silver, four other houses, and her jewelry, she managed to keep three of the seventeen medals she had worn across her bosom in concert, the largest a gold medal from President Hippolyte of the Haitian Republic. "From the top bar, a ribbon holding a bar inscribed Madame Jones and below the medal with Black Patti around the top with a diamond above, and the bottom, Republique-1891-Haiti with a diamond below." When she finally went on relief, the city required her to sign over 7 Wheaton Street. Soon Madame Jones was stricken with cancer. During the last two years of her illness, William P. H. Freeman, a Black realtor and past president of the Providence N.A.A.C.P., paid her estate tax, water tax, wood and coal bill, and other essentials. He also provided the grave in Grace Church Cemetery that kept her remains out of Potter's Field.[77]

Once singled out "as the greatest singer of the race before the public," she was largely forgotten after she left the stage.[78] Sissieretta Jones died penniless 24 June 1933 in the Rhode Island Hospital, Providence, R.I. The obituary in the *Baltimore Afro American* read: "This piece of history is fast passing into discard as one by one, the pioneers of the stage pass on, 'Black Patti' is at the end of her line."[79]

During her years on the concert stage, Mme. Jones sang before a predominantly White audience—"an audience which expected to find a freak, a comical, awkward, unusually strange creature before it, but which found instead an artist who exhibited the same training known to the white singers of her time as well as a decorum which gave her dignity and finesse to the Negro image on the concert stage."[80]

Through her association with the Troubadours, "Madame Jones created a substitute for the legitimate American operatic stage from which she was excluded. The operatic kaleidoscope was a production in which she was able to realize at least partial fulfillment of her artistic inclinations and desires."[81]

Black Patti encountered racial discrimination. Ironically, her efforts to circumvent some of the artistic and cultural restrictions imposed upon her resulted, according to Daughtry, in significant contributions to the further development of the Black artist.

> The very atmosphere which restricted Sissieretta Jones and which destroyed her desire to perform on the Metropolitan stage forced her to make a contribution to American concert and theatrical life – the creation of a musical-dramatic compound which employed both the comical the serious and which gave the Negro a chance to learn the basics of the arts of stagecraft and performance. Without this beginning which Madame Jones' Troubadours provided, there would not have been available – opportunities for the Negro actor to gain experience – opportunities which provided him with rudimentary training in performance as well with an aesthetic attitude toward the American stage.[82]

During the nineteen seasons that "Black Patti's Troubadours" toured the United States and Canada, as in minstrelsy, performers changed frequently. In addition to featuring the star, her shows gave many actors, comedians, singers, and dancers, especially women, the opportunity to work on the professional stage, where they gained "experience in staging and performing which could later be helpful on the larger American stage."[83]

In 1898 "Diminutive Ida 'Topsy' Forsyne" (who had portrayed Topsy in a production of *Uncle Tom's Cabin*) joined "Black Patti's Troubadours." " 'For my specialty,' " said Ida, " 'I pushed a baby carriage across the stage and sang a lullaby, "You're Just a Little Nigger but You're Mine All Mine," and no one thought of objecting in those days.' "[84]

Born in Chicago in 1883, Ida Forsyne (Forcen) Hubbard began dancing professionally in 1893 as a "pick" cakewalking with a Black boy at the Chicago World's Fair, earning 25 cents a day.[85] For several years, she earned considerably more money than her mother cakewalking at cabarets on weekends.[86] At fourteen Ida ran away with a show. It was called *The Bostonians*. When the show went broke in Butte, Montana, she earned her fare home by adopting a five-year-old as a prop and passing his hat as they walked up and down the aisles of railroad cars harmonizing "On the Banks of the Wabash."[87]

Ida learned to dance by watching others. She sharpened her skills while performing with the Troubadours. Black Patti was the only member of the company who had been trained to sing opera. The other members of the troupe were instructed to sing loudly behind Mme. Jones in the finale. In 1902, before this edition of the show closed, Ida's salary was raised to $25.[88]

By 1903 Ida was dancing throughout Europe. Laura Bowman recalled seeing her perform in Vienna at Bal Tabarin, a well-known nightclub. Ida and Laura performed on the same bill in Odessa, Russia. In 1904, when the "Cossacks were riding and cutting heads as they rode," Ida, Laura, and Ida's cousin Ollie Bourgoyne (from *In Dahomey*) were in Moscow. For their safety, they were escorted to a train leaving the country by the American Consul. Ida, Laura, and Ollie returned to the United States together.[89] Shortly afterward, Ida appeared on Broadway at the New York Theatre where she danced a solo in Will Marion Cook's musical, *The Southerners*, which opened on 23 May 1904.[90] Laura Bowman appeared in the chorus.[91] Abbie Mitchell portrayed Mandy Lou, a principal in this integrated show.[92]

Ida "was a very small person of dark brown complexion," commented Bowman. "Her very short hair was not too good a quality. But Ida was not the type to let a little thing like that stop her. She had wigs made out of chestnut curls. When she was made up for her act she looked like a brown doll."[93]

Forsyne reached prominence in 1906 at the Palace Theatre in London. She had returned to Europe in 1905 with "Abbie Mitchell and Her Colored Students." Composed mostly of string musicians and singers, the group was also known as the "Tennessee Students" and the "Memphis Students." The show was a hit, wrote Fletcher. "Ida was a novelty. Her dancing as described by drama critics and show folks was a riot."[94] According to Stearns and Stearns, "Ida Forsyne, judging by a handbill printed at the time, was the star. Her photograph appears on the cover – full faced wearing a bandanna, with an infectious grin. The same picture appeared on magazine covers and in London buses."[95]

After the run of the show, she accepted a long-term contract with the Marinelli Agency (one of the largest theatrical agencies in Europe). She headlined at all the top houses.[96] Ida sang and danced at the Moulin Rouge in Paris that entire first year. Around 1906 she went to London where she introduced her Sack dance at the Alhambra Theatre. A stagehand would appear carrying Ida in a potato sack. She would thrust out an arm, then a leg, the other arm, then the other leg until he had dumped her in the center of the stage. While the music roared, Ida, dressed in a potato sack, would dance "like a wild woman," until a shot rang out, and she fell down and died. Her act also included a chorus of ballet dancers who received extra money to perform in blackface.[97]

Ida performed solo throughout Europe for nine years. Although she was married to Usher Watts, a singer, she and her husband performed separately in different countries. Because Ida was able to imitate what she saw and heard, she sang and spoke in French, German, Russian, and Norwegian. According to Ida, since Black entertainers usually stayed in Europe longer than a year, they learned and brought back some of each country's art and culture. Ida settled in Russia around 1906, where she was the toast of St. Petersburg and Moscow, performing the cakewalk that had been popularized by Williams and Walker. Later, she traveled throughout Russia performing native Russian dances.[98]

In 1914, after living and entertaining in Russia for almost ten years, Ida returned to the United States an expert in Russian dancing.[99] In 1915 she appeared in *Darkydom* at the Lafayette Theatre in New York. In 1919 Ida performed in *Over the Top* at the Grand Theatre in Chicago. Having difficulty finding steady work, Ida danced in a number of musical shows during the 1920s. From 1920 to 1922, she worked for Sophie Tucker earning $50 a week as a maid on and off the stage. Sophie sang and Ida danced at the end of the act. In 1924 she was one of six chorus girls with Mamie Smith's act, and in 1926 she toured the South with a later Smart Set Company.[100]

Upon her return to New York, Ida tried to get work at the major nightclubs such as the Cotton Club, Small's Paradise, and Connie's Inn, "but she was refused because they featured light-skinned chorus girls."[101] Ida recalled that although she got jobs, they were not as good as those in Europe. She believed that she did not make it to the top here because she did not get the opportunity to show what she could do. According to Ida, she did not get that chance because "there's something about my skin that gives me away." By this time, Ida had come to realize that the years she had spent performing in Europe were the pinnacle of her artistic success. Contrasting the response to her talent here with that in Europe, she remarked, "They treated me like a princess."[102]

In 1927, Ida traveled with Bessie Smith's show earning $35 weekly performing a Russian solo and dancing in the chorus. During 1930 she played a bit part in *Lily White;* in 1932 she appeared as Mrs. Noah in *Green Pastures* and in *The Emperor Jones* with Rex Ingram; and in

1935 she was seen in Oscar Micheaux's film, *The Underworld.*[103] In 1938 Forsyne was a member of the congregation of *Conjur,* featuring Laura Bowman.[104] As late as 1951, she assisted Jerome Robbins in choreographing "The Cakewalk" for the New York City Ballet.[105] Ida worked at whatever was available. Writing in the March 1944 issue of *American News,* an American Hotels Corporation publication, a correspondent from Schenectady announced: "We have in our midst a movie actress — Ida Forsyne Hubbard, our new elevator operator."[106] An article in the 23 October 1982 issue of the New York *Amsterdam News* reported

> Ida Hubbard Forsyne, the 121-year old [my sources indicate she would be 97] dancer who was able to lift her legs above her head at the age of 80-plus, is in Concord Baptist Nursing Home in Brooklyn. . . . Ida and the late Dewey Wineglass danced all over the world. She was in Russia during the time of the Czar when, according to Ida, the Czar had a Black girl friend who came from Hell's Kitchen. She remembers the bloody end of the reign of the Czar and how they left a bloody trail. In fact, she recalls her own flight to China and back to the U.S. . . . Ida is always smiling, although she has lost her sight and has been disabled during the past decade.[107]

In spite of the restrictions imposed on a dark-skinned Black female entertainer in America at the turn of the century, she remained in love with show business. "I was born to be a performer," said Ida. Reflecting upon her many experiences in a long and eventful life, Ida remarked humorously, "I'm the happiest uneducated woman you've ever seen."[108] Despite repeated requests to the Concord Baptist Nursing Home, a reply as to whether Ida Forsyne is still alive has not been forthcoming. Ida Forsyne did become an actress in legitimate theatre. She played only minor roles, however.

Dora Dean provided an elegant and sophisticated stage image of a Black woman. She and her husband established several firsts on the professional stage, paving the way for others. Through her shows, she, like Black Patti, gave many singers and dancers the opportunity to work, both here and abroad. Possessing training and talent comparable to her White contemporaries, Sissieretta Jones brought a new dignity to the stage image of Black Americans. Willis Laurence James, a professor at Spelman College, recalled the pride and excitement created by the Troubadours when they arrived in Jacksonville, his home town. "She was a kind of 'racial' heroine because she was so outstanding as a singer," said Professor James, "even by white standards, and white people came to hear her, too."[109] Ida "Topsy" Forsyne headlined at the top theatres in Europe. Through talent, creativity, style, and charm, she provided Europeans with a positive image of Black performers, establishing herself as a role model for others. Although they were admired and accepted throughout the world, especially in Europe, these entertainers were never completely accepted in America.

4

THE EARLY BLACK DRAMATIC
ACTRESS

Mainly, Black women first entered the professional theatre as singers and dancers in musical shows, only later performing in dramatic roles. The women in this chapter illustrate this evolutionary cycle. In fact, Inez Clough appeared in the first recorded dramatic production on the professional legitimate stage in America in which Black actresses were seen. She was born in Worcester, Massachusetts (c. 1860s–70s), and educated in Worcester and Boston. Following the path traveled by Elizabeth Taylor-Greenfield, the Hyers Sisters, and Sissieretta Jones, Clough was trained as a concert singer and pianist. From 1897 to 1906 Clough lived in Europe. During her stay abroad, she was coached in voice in Austria and London.[1] She began receiving attention during the 1880s when she started singing in local concerts in Worcester.

Clough began her professional career performing on the stage in *Oriental America* (1896). She sang in the section entitled "Forty Minutes of Grand and Comic Opera." In 1903, while *In Dahomey* was in London, Clough (who had remained in Europe entertaining after the run of *Oriental America*), joined the chorus.[2] During her nearly ten years abroad, Clough performed solo in the major music halls of the British Isles.[3] While living in London, she played in the English Pantomimes. Two of her roles were as fairy queens and three as a "principal boy" in the musicals *Robinson Crusoe, Red Riding Hood,* and *Dick Whittington.*[4]

In 1906, after Clough had returned to the United States, she joined Cole and Johnson's *Shoo-Fly Regiment.* "Inez Clough," reported the *New York Age,* "made a distinctly favorable impression, her strong soprano voice eliciting much of the applause."[5] During the run of *Shoo-Fly,* she left the show to join Williams and Walker in *Abyssinia* (1907) and then in *Bandana Land* (1908). Clough also appeared as a Flower Girl in the chorus of *Mr. Lode of Koal* (1909), Bert Williams's last all-Black show.[6]

When opportunities in musical theatre became scarce, Clough appeared on the concert stage as a soloist, singing in New York, Washington, and other major cities throughout the East.[7] She toured in vaudeville until she joined the Lafayette Players in 1916.[8] A charter member, she performed in numerous productions at the Lafayette.

During 1916 Clough appeared as Teresa Rand in Clyde Fitch's *The City.* "Anita Bush and Inez Clough divided honors as the two sisters," said the *New York Age.*[9] Clough also played Mrs. Conway in Harold McGrath and Grace Livingston's *The Man on the Box;* Mrs. Edward Ramsey in Channing Pollock's *In the Bishop's Carriage;* Mrs. Sholto in *Sherlock Holmes in Sign of the Four,* an adaptation of Conan Doyle's novel; and Madame Catherine Lockwood in George Scarborough's *The Lure.*[10] According to the *New York Age,* "Inez Clough rises to unsuspected heights as Mme. Catherine Lockwood, conducting the fashionable *demi monde* resort which is the white slavers' headquarters."[11]

In 1917 Clough portrayed Procula, the wife of Pilate, in Ridgley Torrence's *Simon the Cyrenian,* one of *Three Plays for a Negro Theatre.* Louis Sherwin, reviewing for the New York *Globe,* wrote:

> Rarely have I heard such spontaneous enthusiasm in an American theatre. Ordinarily the applause that rewards the actors on first night comes from their personal friends or claque. But there was no such thing last night. The enjoyment of the boxes and the parterre was, for once, as genuine and unrestrained as that of the gallery. . . . The acting, for the most part, was quite inspiring. . . .
>
> "Simon the Cyrenian" was excellently staged. Herein Robert Edmond Jones' skill in scenic design had wider scope. And never have I heard such thrilling, gruesome shouting from a mob. The effect of the procession was achieved with wonderful economy of detail. The acting of Inez Clough, Andrew Bishop, and John T. Butler, which really deserves full comment, was especially impressive.[12]

"In 'The Rider of Dreams' and 'Granny Maumee' there was a display of talent that justified Mrs. Hapgood's strange venture," reported Charles Darnto. He added, " 'Simon the Cyrenian' . . . disclosed little more than the limitations of the actors. Only Inez Clough, as Procula, gave it dramatic life."[13] According to the *New York Age,* "Inez Clough made a stately and sympathetic Procula."[14]

By the time she was cast in the leading female role in *Simon the Cyrenian,* Clough had already garnered twenty years of theatrical experience. This role was a personal triumph for her. George Jean Nathan, a prominent critic, named Clough seventh on his "Ten Best Actresses of the Year" list for 1917.[15]

After *Three Plays* closed, Clough returned to the Lafayette Players where she appeared as Mascha in the comic opera *The Chocolate Soldier;* Lady Henrietta Verdayne in Elinor Glynn's *Three Weeks;* Mme. Dupont in Eugene Brieux's *Damaged Goods;* Sallie Graice in Willie Collier's comedy *The Man from Mexico;* and Dolly Belmar in *Branded.* Other productions in which Clough was seen included the comedies *Are You a Mason?* and *Charlie's Aunt;* Hubert Davies's drama *The Outcast;* Bayard Veiller's *The Flight;* Robert McLaughlin's *The Eternal Magdalene;* Eugene Walter's *Just a Woman;* Cleve Kinkead's *Common Clay;* and the musicals *Song of Songs, A Pair of Queens,* and *The Little Millionaire.*[16]

In 1921 Clough debuted on the screen in *The Simp.* Also in 1921, she was seen in the film *Ties of Blood.* Both films were produced by REOL Productions.[17] In 1922 Clough performed in *Dumb Luck,* a musical. The show, starring Arthur G. Moss and Edward Frye, a successful comedy team (and featuring Alberta Hunter) opened on the road on 11 September in Stamford, Connecticut. Failing to attract the attention of the press and the public, it closed on 23 September in Worcester, Massachusetts, leaving the cast of ninety stranded. At the time, *Shuffle Along* was playing in Boston. When Messrs. Blake, Miller, Lyles, and Sissle (stars and producers of the show), heard of the financial problems, they offered financial assistance to Moss (who was also co-producer). Moss, however, refused the offer. When arrangements had not been made by the following Saturday, William C. Elkins, director of the chorus, called Noble Sissle and told him of the situation. Despite Moss's previous refusal, the producers of *Shuffle Along* sent Mrs. Sissle to Worcester with $400, which enabled fifty members of the *Dumb Luck* company to return to New York City. Soon afterward, an additional $300 was sent and the remainder of the cast was able to return to New York.[18] In 1924 Clough played the part of Mrs. Hez Brown, the wife, in *Chocolate Dandies* at the Colonial Theatre in New York. This musical, which featured Josephine Baker, was created jointly by Eubie Blake and Noble Sissle.[19]

Returning to drama Clough played the lead, Deborah, in Em Jo Basshe's *Earth,* first produced on 9 February 1927 by the "militant theatre group" The New Playwrights Theatre in their theatre on Fifty-second Street.[20] The show ran there for twenty-six performances.[21] On 21 March 1927 *Earth* moved to the Grove Street Theatre where it played until 2 April 1927.[22] *Earth* depicts the conflict between Christianity and Voodoo among rural Blacks during the 1880s. Percy Hammond of the *Herald-Tribune* said, "Miss Inez Clough exerts noticeable talents for emotional acting as Deborah."[23] According to the New York *Graphic*, "Inez Clough, the grief-stricken and blasphemous Deborah in the play, gave an uncommonly fine performance. . . ."[24] Brooks Atkinson, reviewing for *The New York Times*, wrote: "the rich voices of Mr. Hayes and Miss Clough in the leading parts soothe the ear quite apart from what they say."[25] An article in the New York *Amsterdam News*, entitled "Inez Clough Scores Remarkable Hit at Playwrights' Theatre," reported: "The chief feature of the evening was the stirring acting of Inez Clough as Deborah. She revealed herself to be an emotional actress of splendid ability. . . . Her performance last Thursday night was deeply moving."[26]

On 2 July 1928 Clough opened in Don Mullally's comedy *Wanted* at the Wallack Theatre in New York for sixteen performances.[27] Staged by Mullally, *Wanted* is about a White girl from a good family who moves to New York from Baton Rouge. When her money runs out, she is invited to stay temporarily in the Park Avenue apartment of a couple who are in Europe. Although she does not know the couple, she knows the two Black maids from Baton Rouge. Before she leaves, the couple returns and a robbery occurs. The couple's nephew falls in love with the girl, the thief is caught, and all ends well. "Teresa Brooks and Inez Clough, both colored, who act the maids, handle important roles flawlessly," noted *The Evening World*.[28]

On 20 February 1929, Clough opened in Jourdon Rapp and Wallace Thurman's *Harlem*, "An Episode of Life in New York's Black Belt" at the Apollo Theatre in New York for ninety-four performances.[29] A melodrama, *Harlem* tells the story of Cordelia Williams, a girl from a small southern town, who goes wrong north of 125th Street. In a cast of seventy-four Blacks and one White, Clough played Ma Williams. The reviewer for the *New York Times* wrote, "Inez Clough, as the mother of a scrabbling family, has gentleness and dignity in her acting."[30] The *Herald Tribune* said, "Inez Clough was sincere and moving as the uprooted and bewildered mother."[31]

Also in 1929, Clough was one of the stars of Jeroline Hemsely's first play, *Wade in de Water*, at the Cherry Lane Theatre in New York City. Presented by the New Negro Art Theatre, *Wade in de Water* is set on a plantation in Georgia in 1885. It violently depicts the White man's antipathy towards Blacks. "Inez Clough and Hemsely Winfield are to be considered apart from the rest of the cast by virtue of professional experience. 'Wade in de Water' derives its title from the spiritual which holds out hope for divine intervention," noted the *New York Times*.[32]

The 28 May 1930 *New York Times* provided a review of a once-performed piece called *De Promis' Lan'*. This two-act, twelve-scene pageant, with dialogue by Jeroline Hemsely and score by Russell Wooding, was presented by the National Negro Pageant Association of Chicago at Carnegie Hall in New York City. Inez Clough played one of the principal parts in this epic. Of the show, the reviewer wrote: "In failing to be impressive at the same time that it was serious, 'De Promis' Lan' ' only followed in the path of most similar attempts, which are content to drowse until it is time to sing and dance. . . . A few spirituals were harshly and insufficiently rendered, and the voices of de promis' lan', in chorus and quartet numbers, proved to be less divine than in need of rehearsal."[33]

Beginning in November 1930, NBC radio presented a weekly play of "life among colored folk" on Sundays at 2:15 P.M. F. Carlton Moss was the author and one of the featured actors. The show ran for over a year. During this period, Inez Clough appeared in the cast of players.[34]

On 31 December 1931 Harry Hamilton and Norman Foster's *Savage Rhythm* opened at the John Golden Theatre for 12 performances.[35] A drama of Black sorcery, *Savage Rhythm* takes place down South in the village of "Tuckaloo" where superstitions, magic, and self-hypnosis are accepted as part of the Christian religion. During a lively barbecue, one of the "Conjur-Woman's" granddaughters (a singer visiting from Harlem played by Vivian Barber) is fatally stabbed by the wife of the adulterous "Sweetback" with whom she has been partying. Inez Clough portrayed "Sweetback's Wife," her last recorded role on the stage. "Restraint and comprehension are in Miss Clough's interpretation," wrote Robert Garland of the *World Telegraph*.[36] Burns Mantle, reviewing for the *Daily News*, said, "The acting is as simple and effective as the play itself. There are excellent performances . . . especially by Inez Clough, the unhappy wife who stabs a cheating husband as a service to the Lord."[37] "Credits also to Vivian Barber as the star, Venezuela Jones as the sister, Inez Clough, Juano Hernandez and Mamie Cartier," said the *Chicago Defender.*[38] Some critics gave unfavorable reviews. "The acting of the Negro cast is shapeless and uneven," wrote Brooks Atkinson. " 'Savage Rhythm' has only its intelligence and temperament."[39]

Clough was last seen on the screen in *The Crimson Fog* (1932), produced by Charles Allman White.[40] On 24 November 1933, after a long illness, Clough died in Cook County Hospital in Chicago. "Inez Clough is no more," eulogized the *Amsterdam News*. "The voice which William Faversham, the celebrated actor, said was one of the best he ever heard, is silent." Clough was survived by her estranged husband, Harry P. Hogan.[41]

By performing in musicals, dramas, and film (whenever opportunity permitted), Inez Clough was able to piece together a career that lasted

more than a quarter of a century. She performed in two landmark productions that made theatrical history: *Oriental America* (1896) and
Three Plays for a Negro Theatre (1917). Further, these presentations
were extremely important for the Black female performer; they gave
her prominence and stature. Clough made the theatre her lifelong career. Her rise from chorus girl to dramatic actress was not an isolated
phenomenon; rather, it appears to reflect the pattern of development
common to other Black women who also made the successful transition
from musicals to dramas.

On 18 June 1904 Robert Motts, a Black restaurant owner, opened the
Pekin Theatre, located on 27th and State Streets in Chicago, Illinois.
Originally the Pekin served as a vaudeville theatre and music hall. Due
to a fire in 1905, Motts renovated the theatre; he enlarged the stage
and added a balcony. In an attempt to make the Pekin a popular family
theatre, in 1906 Motts began presenting musical comedy, establishing
the "first legitimate Black theatre in the United States." Advertised as
"the only first-class and properly equipped theatre in the United States
owned, managed and controlled by colored promoters," the Pekin featured Black artists exclusively. Producing original musical shows required a large cast. The Pekin Stock Company evolved out of the need
created by changing the bill every two weeks. During the early part of
1911, the Pekin Stock Company was disbanded. Soon after, the theatre
became a vaudeville house. In July 1911, Bob Motts died.[42] Like the
Lafayette Players several years later, the Pekin Players provided valuable training and experience for a number of actresses who went on to
perform professionally in both musicals and dramas on the New York
stage. Among these were Abbie Mitchell and Lottie Grady.

Before sharing the lead with Bert Williams in *Mr. Lode of Koal* (1909)
on Broadway, Lottie Grady (a singer and dancer) had been a member of
the Pekin Players. In 1899, years before joining the Pekin Players,
Grady toured with Charles P. Trux's 400 Company. She was first seen
at the Pekin as the Belle of San Domingo in the musical *The Grafters*
(1907). Featuring music by Joe Jordan and Tim Bryan, the play deals
with the problems of Reuben Easy, a prosperous businessman who
gets involved with a stranded opera company. In April 1907 she performed in *Doctor Dope*. An original musical comedy, *Doctor Dope* depicts the troubles of "Hotstetter Dope" (nicknamed "Hot Dope"), an
illiterate but good-hearted man who is mistaken for a noted physician.[43]

During that same month, she appeared in a musical comedy, *The
Husband*. Written by Flournoy E. Miller and Aubrey Lyles, the future
co-stars and co-creators of *Shuffle Along* (1921), *The Husband* featured
music by Joe Jordon. Also in 1907 Grady played the Filipino Girl in
Captain Rufus, a military musical. In August of that year, the Pekin

Players presented *Captain Rufus* and *The Husband* at Hurtig and Seamon's Music Hall Theatre in New York for two weeks. Grady played the Wife in the 1909 edition of *The Husband* presented at the Pekin. She was Phonia in the musical *Merry Widower* (1908) and Lucy Johnson in *Simple Mollie* (1908), both at the Pekin. In *Simple Mollie* Grady sang "Taffy Finally."[44]

In March 1909 Grady played Nora Smith in Irvin C. (brother of Flournoy) Miller's *The Man Upstairs* at the Pekin. In April she was Ada Norton in *The Chambermaid,* an adaptation of the French farce *Jane.* During the same month, she appeared as Mrs. Helen Harding in *The Idlers.* The cast also included Charles Gilpin and Lawrence Chenault.[45]

On 1 November 1909 *Mr. Lode of Koal,* starring Bert Williams, opened at the Majestic Theatre in New York City where it ran for forty performances.[46] A three-act musical by J. A. Shipp and Alexander Rogers, with music by J. Rosamond Johnson, *Mr. Lode of Koal* takes place on the mythical island of Koal. Big Smoak, the ruler, is kidnapped, and Chester A. Lode is forced to take his place. In the end the king returns, and he condemns Chester to being one of his servants. Lottie Grady played Mysteria.[47]

Before opening on Broadway, *Mr. Lode of Koal* previewed at the Great Northern Theatre in Chicago. The critic suggested some changes before the play reached New York:

> The mistake that Mr. Williams has made in this new venture is that he has failed to have his people placed in the cast to his own advantage, and to fill the vacancies left by the absence of Mr. and Mrs. Walker. In failing to do this, both his partner, George W. Walker, and Aida Overton Walker are naturally missed. . . . Miss Lottie Grady, . . . who is fully capable as an all-around actress, should have been given full sway, . . . She was sweet to look upon, but had little to do, and made much out of a small scene with Mr. Williams. She will probably have more to do when Mr. Williams finds out that she is expected by the public to fill the place left vacant by Aida Overton Walker. . . . To be plain, the show is badly regulated. It needs a female classical soloist in the worst way, and I fancy if Mr. Williams does not utilize the full force of talented people in his company, he may see frost before winter.[48]

Despite calling the plot a "jumble of nonsense and music," the *New York Times* printed a favorable review: "Bert Williams is fully as amusing by himself as he was as a part of the partnership of Williams and Walker. . . . The chorus has the vocal vigor and quality to be expected

4. Lottie Grady and her partner, Sherman H. Dudley, in their vaudeville act (1912). Photo courtesy of The Billy Rose Theatre Collection, The New York Public Library for the Performing Arts, Astor, Lenox and Tilden Foundations.

of negro singers, and its members seem to enjoy their work. The soloists, too, are proficient in voice and expression. . . ."[49]

The reviewer for the *Indianapolis Freeman* commented that "Miss Grady looked the part and acted the part, showing her to be a finished artist in every sense of the word." He added, "Miss Grady sang 'Mum's the Word, Mr. Moore.' The song took three good, solid encores, and Miss Grady can rest assured she captured Broadway."[50]

Grady played Lillie White in the 1910 edition of *His Honor the Barber,* starring S. H. Dudley and Ada Walker.[51] In 1911 she was seen in *Dr. Herb's Prescription; or, It Happened in a Dream* at the Pekin. An adaptation of *Mr. Lode of Koal, Dr. Herb's Prescription,* a farce with music, was also written by J. A. Shipp. Grady, who played Mysteria the Soothsayer (the same role she had created in *Mr. Lode of Koal*), sang "Mums the Word Mr. Moore."[52] Also in 1911 Grady appeared in another musical, *The Lime Kiln Club,* also at the Pekin.[53] Grady also performed at the Pekin in *Physco Gasarino.* She played Miss Dollie Dot and sang "Kiss Me."[54] In 1913 she was seen there in Flournoy Miller and Aubrey Lyles's musical *The Cabaret.* In 1915 Grady appeared in Irvin C. Miller's first hit show, *Broadway Rastus.* Featuring music by W. C. Handy, *Broadway Rastus* opened at the Apollo Theatre in Atlantic City, N.J.[55]

In 1917 Grady joined the Lafayette Players.[56] According to Anita Bush, "Lottie played ladies' parts."[57] (No information regarding roles was found.) Before joining the Lafayette Players, Grady had been anticipating making the transition from musicals to dramas. She had been a member of the dramatic class of the Pekin Stock Company where she played Stella Darbisher in C. Haddon Chambers's four-act drama *Captain Swift. Captain Swift* was the "first dramatic effort of the Dramatic school of acting under the tutorship of Mr. [J. Ed.] Green," announced an undated handbill.[58]

Two weeks prior to the opening of *Three Plays,* the role of Acte, Princess of Egypt in *Simon the Cyrenian* had not been cast. Numerous actresses auditioned for the part, but none was acceptable. According to Lester Walton, in an article entitled "In Quest of Egyptian Princess":

Some of our belles who would win a prize in a beauty contest have failed to land the coveted role because of inability to read lines like a real actress. Others had sparkled as elocutionists but fallen short of what an Egyptian princess is expected to possess in the way of personal charm; then there have been instances where the applicant could act and was pronounced "a thing of beauty" but was told her color was not in keeping with the part. So with opening night only a few weeks off the search for the Egyptian princess goes merrily on.

P.S. – The "Egyptian Princess" has been found in the person of Miss Lottie Grady, rated as one of the race's most talented performers. Miss Grady received her education in the dramatic art as a member of the famous Pekin Stock Company. She has played leading parts with our largest colored musical productions.[59]

On 5 April 1917 Grady portrayed Acte, Princess of Egypt in *Simon the Cyrenian,* one of the *Three Plays* on Broadway. Rennold Wolf, reviewing for the New York *Telegraph,* wrote:

To be sure, the spectacle of stage boxes filled with negroes in evening dress, is not usual at New York first night performances, nor was the sprinkling of blacks in the lobby and the first rows of the balcony. Yet everyone present accepted the endeavor in good faith, and followed the proceedings attentively and respectfully. . . . The most pretentious production of the bill is "Simon the Cyrenian," . . . An extremely simply but none the less effective setting shows the garden of Pilate's house. Otherwise there is little impressive about the play, save that it is acted earnestly and after the fashion of classic stilted drama. John T. Butler looks an imposing Simon, but plays the role indifferently. Lottie Grady acts the Princess with some distinction.[60]

The New York *American* said of *Simon the Cyrenian:* "The chief honors went to John T. Butler, as Simon; Lottie Grady, as the Princess of Egypt; and Inez Clough as the wife of Pilate."[61] "Inez Clough, John T. Butler and Lottie Grady in 'Simon the Cyrenian' were splendidly capable," commented one reviewer.[62] The *New York Age* said, "Lottie Grady was admirably cast for the emotional role of Acte, Princess of Egypt."[63] Acte, Princess of Egypt is the last recorded role performed by Grady. The apparent gap in her biography is mainly due to one of two reasons: (1) What she was doing was not documented, or (2) She dropped out of show business and was not involved with performance. The date of Grady's death has not been established.

"In 1915, Anita Bush introduced Negro drama in New York City," according to Henry T. Sampson, "by organizing the Colored Dramatic Stock Company which she later renamed the Anita Bush Stock Company."[64] Sister Francesca Thompson credited Bush with bringing the first permanent stock company to the Lafayette Theatre. Bush, the daughter of a tailor whose clientele was mostly show people, was born in Washington, D.C. (c. 1887), but grew up in Brooklyn, New York. As children, she and her sister played "extra serving maids" in *Anthony and Cleopatra* presented by a group of White professionals at the Park Theatre in New York. She recalled appearing in every scene possible and learning all of the other actors' lines. After their "debut," she and her sister played every part given to them whenever they could manage to beg or wheedle the leading actors, manager, or director to hire them.[65] "We felt certain," said Bush, "that Broadway didn't know what talents it was missing."[66]

In 1903, when Bush was sixteen, Bert Williams persuaded her father to permit her to join the chorus of *In Dahomey*. When her father questioned Williams about his reasons for hiring Bush (who was supposedly untalented), Williams tactfully replied, " 'Oh, she'll make a pretty picture on stage.' "[67] Bush remained with Williams and Walker for six years, until 1909, when the company disbanded.[68] During that time, Bush was one of Ada Walker's "special dancers."[69]

Out of work, Bush selected four or five of the most talented chorus girls from the company and formed her own dancing troupe. They performed on the music hall circuit until 1913 when Bush injured her back in a serious accident backstage. While recuperating, she decided to form a dramatic stock company. After attending a Saturday matinee of a silent film at the newly renovated Lincoln Theatre in Harlem (with only five or six patrons present), Bush approached Eugene "Frenchy" Elmore, the manager, with her concept. Due to a slump in business, Elmore agreed, hoping to increase the box office receipts. A finished performance was to be presented in two weeks. Bush signed a contract formalizing the Anita Bush Stock Company.[70]

On 15 November 1915 Bush and her troupe, including Carlotta Freeman and Charles Gilpin, opened at the Lincoln with Billie Burke's farcical comedy *The Girl at the Fort*. Burke, a White actress and author, also directed the piece. Bush, who had recently recovered from pneumonia, recalled opening night:

> I was the happiest, sick ingenue in the whole world. All of the best people, some of whom had never crossed the sill of the Lincoln Theatre before, were there to welcome us. The house was packed and so were the sidewalks outside. Everything went off like clockwork. Everyone knew his lines and not a single mistake was made. I shall never forget or cease to be grateful for the reception given us by the people of Harlem, our own people. I laugh whenever I hear myself called "The Little Mother of [Negro] Drama." No one will ever know what labor pains were borne by the "Little Mother" that week before the show opened, plus the job of learning my lines for my part as the Girl at the Fort. But on opening night I knew it was worth every agony I had suffered.[71]

The press was very favorable to these neophyte actors. Of Bush's performance, an unidentified clipping from her scrapbook reported: "Anita Bush, our charmingly petite 'Lady of the Dances,' demonstrated her versatility and ability to jump from one extreme to the other. Popular as she has been in her dances, she lost none of that popularity by entering the ranks of the drama, but is even more popular, if possible, for her delightful delineation of Clarice, the girl at the fort."[72]

The response of the community to the performance was so overwhelming that Mrs. Marie C. Downs, the proprietor of the Lincoln, prompted by the prospect of capitalizing on a good business venture, demanded that Bush change the name of the group to the Lincoln Players. Bush refused, gave two weeks' notice, and moved her company of five to the rival Lafayette Theatre, taking the newly acquired audience with her. On 27 December 1915 the group premiered there with *Across the Footlights*, starring Bush.[73] Interestingly, the name was soon changed to the Lafayette Players. "Apparently, Anita Bush was no longer adamant about her name being used," noted Sister Thompson, "because in spite of the changed name, Miss Bush remained with the Players until 1920."[74]

During the first three months of 1916 the Lafayette Players presented the following plays, and Anita Bush appeared in most of them: *The Gambler's Sweetheart*, "borrowed" from David Belasco's *The Girl of the Golden West; The Octoroon; New York After Dark; Wanted—A Family; When the Wife's Away; Roanoke; Southern Life; For His Daughter's Honor; The World Against Him; Within the Law;* and *Paid in Full.*[75]

The patrons supported these new players. During a three-week period, Bush and her troupe of five were paid over \$1,300 in salary. Although they enjoyed the productions offered, this Harlem audience began to complain that the material was too "White." In response to their demands, Bush initiated a contest for the best sixty-minute sketch dealing with Black life.[76] Since no Black plays were presented, it appears that the playwriting contest did not produce suitable works.

The fame of the Lafayette Players spread throughout the country. In April 1916 Bush received an offer to form a stock company in Chicago. This was not to be a rival company, but an extension of the New York company. Bush premiered with *The Girl at the Fort* under the direction of Edgar Forrest at the Grand Theatre in Chicago.[77] The *Indianapolis Freeman* said: "If we are to judge from the verdict given to the first opening . . . it was a good omen . . . the audience was entirely in its favor."[78] Although Chicago had had Black theatricals, they had not been of the type presented by the Lafayette Players. As with the Lincoln and Lafayette theatres in New York, Bush had brought a new sophistication to the Grand Theatre.

By July 1916, besides the Lafayette Players in New York and Chicago, there were companies playing in Baltimore, Washington, D.C., and Philadelphia, plus one in rehearsal for touring. Bush usually played with the touring company, but she performed in New York occasionally.[79] In August 1916, Bush starred in *The Bishop's Carriage* at the Howard Theatre in Washington, D.C. Although this production did not receive the support of the press or the public, Bush's performance was commended:

Miss Anita Bush, the originator of the present dramatic renaissance in the arena of colored theatricals, appeared to advantage as Nance Olden, giving the role a piquant attractiveness and convincing pathos that won the sympathy of her audience from beginning as the confirmed thief to the final curtain when she had learned how to "get diamonds honestly" and had been redeemed by the sacrificial love of a good man. Miss Bush is not an actress of the heavy emotional type, but is an ingenue of strong dramatic promise and one who will make good in parts that call for a dainty touch of the human element spiced with a bit of rollicking comedy. She has proper appraisement of her range of abilities. She has made an excellent impression so far, and is sure of a warm welcome at the hands of our exacting theatregoers.[80]

In October 1916 the Lafayette Players presented *The Lure* in New York. "The acting of Miss Inez Clough, Mr. Andrew Bishop, Will Cooke and the rest of the cast is well done. As for Miss Bush, we do not see how there could be very much improvement in her way of playing 'the girl,'" wrote the *Indianapolis Freeman*.[81]

In a very short time, Bush, a forerunner of Black repertory theatre, achieved one of her lifetime goals. "It had long been a dormant dream of hers," said Sister Francesca Thompson, "to form a legitimate stock company of Black actors to prove to Whites and Blacks alike that Black performers could be successful in some type of theater work other than the 'stereotype-comic-song-and-dance' routines to which theater-goers of the early 1900's were accustomed."[82]

Bush remained with the Lafayette Players until 1920, when she took advantage of other opportunities. In 1921 she starred with Bill Pickett in the first all-Black western film, *The Crimson Skull*, produced by the Norman Brothers.[83] During the same period she starred in two other westerns, *Girl of the Golden West* and *The Bulldogger*.[84] The Bulldogger (1923), produced by Normal Film Manufacturing Company, featured "trick riding by black cowboys and cowgirls."[85]

During the 1920s and 1930 Bush traveled throughout the country with her own company, performing drama, music, and comedy. Her troupes numbered between ten and twenty performers who were paid $50 weekly.[86]

On 22 July 1937 Bush appeared in the WPA's production of *Swing It* at the Adelphi Theatre in New York for sixty performances.[87] A musical written by Cecil Mack, Milton Reddie, and Eubie Blake, *Swing It* is "about a showboat troupe in the South which wants to go to fabulous Harlem." Anita Bush played Amy. The reviewer for the *New York Times* reported: "*Swing It* is a pot-pourri of minstrelsy, singing, dancing, mugging, clowning, spirituals, jazz, swing, tapping and the carrying of Harlem's throaty torch. Dozens of Negro players are taking part, in specialty numbers, in clogging, in buck and wing. Harlem is right down town, having fun in an infectious manner."[88]

Rosetta LeNoire began her professional career during the late 1920s as a teenager touring during the summers with her godfather and dance instructor Bill "Bojangles" Robinson as one of his "Time Steppers," a chorus of twelve dancing girls. Her mentor and voice teacher was Eubie Blake.[89] LeNoire went on to perform in several successful musicals and dramas. She is currently seen on television as the grandmother in ABC's "Family Matters."

According to LeNoire (who also performed in WPA productions), during the 1930s and 1940s Bush was teaching acting at the Harlem "Y." "Anita, I felt, was an overlooked person. She was a brilliant actress and she was a *hell of a good teacher*! When I entered the theatre," she recalled, "acting in dramatic roles was more respected than singing and dancing." At the time LeNoire (who was associated with singing and dancing), was not an official member of the class. She would, however, slip in quietly, sit at the back of the room, and observe Bush. "I would write down everything I saw and heard," she revealed. "In case I got a character to play, I could go back and look up my notes."[90]

In order to supplement her income, for several years – as a young woman and a middle-aged woman – Bush endorsed Kashmir Preparation, a skin whitener and cleanser. Bush, who retired from the stage in 1943, headed her last traveling company in 1941. For several years she was Executive Secretary of the Negro Actors Guild.[91] On 19 February 1974, Bush died at the age of 91 in her Bronx apartment in New York City. She is buried in the Mt. Hope Cemetery in Hastings, New York.[92]

Bush, a pivotal figure in the evolution of the Black theatre-artist, is credited with initiating the careers of more than fifty Black performers.[93] Inez Clough, Lottie Grady, Laura Bowman, Abbie Mitchell, and Bush all gained recognition and valuable experience while acting with the Lafayette Players. Bush's accomplishments have assured her a unique place in the history of American Theatre. Sister Thompson, the daughter of two former stars of the Lafayette Players, Evelyn Preer

5. Anita Bush (1937) performed in *In Dahomey* (1903), *Abyssinia* (1906), and *Mr. Lode of Koal* (1909). Known as "Little Mother of Negro Drama," she formed the Anita Bush Stock Company in 1915, which later became the celebrated Lafayette Players. She costarred in the first all-Black western film, *The Crimson Skull* (1921). Photo courtesy of Hatch-Billops Collection, Inc.

and Edward Thompson, sums up why this Black Theatre "legend" should be remembered:

> Anita Bush's contributions to the success of the Lafayette Players should not be minimized. Without her, there would not have been a company; without her, the company would not have continued to thrive and to grow during the first difficult years of establishment. The company was her idea, her dream, her ambition brought to life. Credit must be given to one who, through her determination, kept the dream alive. Anita Bush's inspiration encouraged others to follow in her footsteps along a previously untraveled path. It was a path that was to lead ultimately to an unparalleled position for black performers in the theatrical world.[94]

"No history of the Negro in the twentieth century theatre can be complete without the name of Laura Bowman," wrote Dido Johnson in an article entitled "The Truly Startling Story of Laura Bowman."[95] Like Anita Bush, Bowman began her professional career in *In Dahomey* (1902). Born of mixed parents (a mulatto father and a Dutch mother) on 3 October 1881 in Quincy, Illinois, but raised in Cincinnati, Laura Bradford started singing as a youngster in church choirs. In 1898, at sixteen, she married Henry Ward Bowman, a railroad porter. She realized that she wanted to sing professionally in 1900 while performing in an Easter program in church. Her memoir, *Achievement: The Life of Laura Bowman,* gave valuable information about her life and career. However, Bowman mentioned few dates. She recalled auditioning in 1902 for Williams and Walker at Heuchs Opera House in Cincinnati. Although she was not hired, because they had enough contract players, they encouraged her. The next week, when the show was returning from Louisiana on its way to Chicago, the advance men hired her for *In Dahomey.* The show played two nights in Des Moines and three nights in Omaha before arriving in Chicago. While there, Laura stayed with Paul Laurence Dunbar and his mother.[96]

In the overture of *In Dahomey* she wore dark grease paint. ("I have always had to use dark makeup so, of course, I had to learn to perfect it," revealed Laura.[97]) She also wore an "ugly-nappy, bushy African wig" and a colorful costume.[98] "We girls had to hide behind big rocks. The floor was covered with grass mats. . . . All we had to do was play hide and seek behind the rocks while Bert Williams, our star, played with us. Our biggest job," remembered Bowman, "was to place ourselves so that we could see Will Marion Cook, our musical director."[99] Hatti McIntosh (who also performed) and Mrs. Reed, Ada Walker's mother, were wardrobe mistresses.[100]

They traveled by train – an entire car for the company – with a banner stretching the length of the car that read "Williams and Walker Company." In 1903 the cast of eighty-one booked second class on the Cunard Line, sailed from New York for England. They rehearsed all day and performed at night. On the way over, "the ghost walked." This was an expression used by Black performers to mean that they were getting paid. Laura received a salary of $18 for two weeks, which was $1 over her original contract.[101]

Pete Hampton, one of the executives and stars of the show who had fallen in love with Laura, taught her to play the banjo. They wrote a couple of songs, formed a vaudeville act, "Hampton and Bowman," and entertained on board. Laura, who said that she was never a good dancer, sang "Swanee River"; together they sang "Lindy" and "Brownskin Baby Mine." They were well received, and she was a hit. After using "Lindy," one of their songs, in the act for several years, Pete and Laura sold it to Johnson and Dean before it was published by a Hungarian music company in Budapest.[102]

The ship landed in Liverpool where the cast took the train to London. *In Dahomey* was one of six shows presenting a command performance for the Prince of Wales's ninth birthday. The acts did not go to the front gate at Buckingham Palace; they had to go to the side gate, then walk about ten blocks. Bowman did not know whether it was because of race.[103] "The sensational part of our show to the English public," said Laura, "was the high cakewalk which gained a tremendous amount of publicity and popularity."[104]

The first company of *In Dahomey* broke up in London in 1903. A new company was formed with Avery and Hart (a comic duo) replacing Williams and Walker. Laura and Pete, however, decided not to join the second company. Instead they formed a quartet, the Darktown Entertainer, featuring William Garland, tenor; Fred Douglas, bass; Pete Hampton, baritone; and Laura, soprano. They sang everything from grand opera to lullabies. Laura was the official representative for the group. They were booked in Leipzig, Germany, at the Crystal Palace by the Shereck and Braff agency, who remained with Hampton and Bowman for twelve years. The Darktown Entertainers performed in Hungary, Austria, France, Russia, Switzerland, and the Balkan countries. Their act was a novelty. Garland sang "Flower Song." While he held a note for three minutes, they passed out roses to the women in the audience. Pete played three numbers on the banjo and harmonica. Then Pete and Laura performed a character sketch. Laura had six character

changes; two were supposed to be overdressed. The act closed with the
Sextette from "Lucia."[105] Bowman's "characterizations in costume" provided training she would eventually use on the dramatic stage.

In Budapest, they were met by two open carriages and a brass band
that rode through town with a banner that read "Darktown Entertainers." During their fifteen-day engagement, they played in an open-air
theatre with canvas on the sides. Laura sang "Swanee River" and
dressed like an old woman. The group played three weeks in Germany
and thirty days in Vienna. While in Vienna, they met Ida Forsyne; she
was dancing at Bal Tabarin, an elegant nightclub.[106]

Both the Darktown Entertainers and Ida were going to Russia; Ida
had already been there. They promised to meet. According to Laura,
Black acts in Europe remained in contact. Their first night in Russia,
the Darktown Entertainers performed on a bill with eleven other acts,
including Hungarian, German, Russian, and French women's choruses.
They did not go on until 10:00 P.M. While in Russia, they met the novel-
ist Leo Tolstoi. Although they were not aware of it, the group was expected to entertain at private parties. While at one of the parties,
Tolstoi offered them 100 rubles to sing "Simple Simon," but no one
could remember the melody. After thirty minutes of singing other
songs, Laura had an idea.[107] "I had a little comedy number I did alone.
It interested him enough to make him at least listen to us, not because
the number was so wonderful but simply because I was a woman."[108]
The group sang for a half hour longer without a break and earned the
100 rubles. However, they felt very cheap and disappointed.[109]

Pete and Laura also performed as a duo while they were members of
the Darktown Entertainers. In Odessa, Laura and Pete were booked on
the same bill with Ida Forsyne. Ida's cousin Ollie Burgoyne (who had
remained in Europe after the run of *In Dahomey*) also accompanied
them to Odessa, but only to vacation. As the political turmoil esca-
lated, the American consul told all Americans to leave Russia. The
Darktown Entertainers and Ida and Ollie (who spoke fluent Russian)
left Russia for London. They were escorted to the train by the consul
and a guard of soldiers.[110] "In those days, to be an American meant
something," said Bowman.[111]

After leaving Russia, the Darktown Entertainers broke up. Ida, Pete,
and Laura booked passage on the *Lusitania* to the United States. The
trip home was only for a visit. The couple had their return tickets to
London and two years of advance bookings awaiting them.[112] On 23
May 1904 Will Marion Cook's musical *The Southerners* opened at the
New York Theatre for thirty-six performances.[113] Ida, Pete, and Laura
were in the company. According to Bowman, "it was strictly an ofay
[White] show although it had a colored chorus."[114]

6. Darktown Entertainers (c. 1904).

After the close of *The Southerners,* Bowman returned to London as a principal in the second company of *In Dahomey,* featuring Avery and Hart. She played Mrs. Lightfoot, Pete's wife. Laura received an $8 raise for doing two parts, singing and acting. Now that she was a principal, and no longer a chorus girl, her stature with the show changed; she received better accommodations and dressing room. This was not a real acting part for Laura. "I already knew the part better than the woman who had been doing it for the past seven months," said Bowman.[115] After the run of *In Dahomey II,* Laura and Pete performed as a duo throughout Europe. They worked in Berlin, Moscow, Prague, Budapest, Rome, Naples, Switzerland, and twenty-six weeks in England. By October 1907 (on her birthday), the couple was back performing in Vienna.[116]

By 1910 Pete and Laura had bought a house in England, and both her parents were living with them. On 20 July 1912 Laura's mother died. Sometime afterward, the English government ordered all foreigners home. The couple returned to New York. They toured the East Coast performing as a duo. On a return trip from Boston, Pete became seriously ill. By this time, Ida Forsyne had returned to the United States. She stayed with Pete and Laura at their 136th Street apartment in Harlem where she helped Laura take care of Pete. Shortly afterward, he died.[117]

In March 1916 Bowman joined the Lafayette Players. At her first rehearsal for Eugene Walker's *The Wolf,* she met Sidney Kirkpatrick. Laura played the part of a Canadian backwoods girl and Sidney was an American engineer in love with her. Only a few days after Pete's death, Laura fell in love with Sidney. Pete Hampton had been several years older than Laura, more of a father and teacher. Sidney and Laura, however, were lovers.[118]

Soon the Lafayette Players numbered about forty. Laura was classified as a "character woman" with the group. Her audiences seemed to enjoy her in tender, motherly parts.[119] That first season Bowman portrayed Martha Washington Johnson in Robert Baker and John Emerson's detective story *The Conspiracy;* Mrs. Dole in George Broadhurst's *The Price;* and Mrs. Blount in Daniel Carter's *The Master Mind.*[120] "Miss Bowman as Mrs. Blount, alias Milwaukee Sadie, the shoplifter, gave a good characterization," said Lucien White of the *New York Age.*[121] Bowman played Rose in *Madame X.* "Miss Laura Bowman as Rose maintained her most excellent reputation as an interpreter of character parts," said White.[122] She was also seen in Bayard Veiller's *Within the Law, Deep Purple, Dr. Jekyll and Mr. Hyde, Today,* and A. Alston's *Tennessee's Pardner.*[123]

The musicals presented during that season included *Fifty Miles from*

Boston, Prince of Pilsen, Hit the Deck, Madam Sherry, Three Twins, A Pair of Sixes, Here Comes the Bride, Chocolate Soldier, Faust, and *Forty-Five Minutes from Broadway,* starring Abbie Mitchell.[124] Reviewing Bowman's performance in *Forty-Five Minutes from Broadway,* White said, "Miss Bowman's voice was heard to good advantage in 'Dreaming,' but the song was hardly suited to the character which she is interpreting."[125]

Other productions in which Bowman was seen include Joseph E. Howard's *The Time, The Place, and the Girl,* C. T. Dazey and Alathea Layson's *In Old Kentucky,* the Wife in *A Fool There Was,* Mrs. Jordon in *The Great Divide,* Mrs. Kate Desmond in Owen Davis's *A Man's Game,* Mrs. Fielding in *The Yankee Prince,* and doubled as Mrs. Meyer and Mrs. Smalley in Jack Lait's *Help Wanted.*[126]

Eventually Laura and Sidney left the Lafayette Players to get married. The management did not want either married couples or sweethearts because "we would lose our value to him unless we remained single," said Bowman.[127] They formed an act and played in Boston, Philadelphia, Washington, and Indianapolis. Laura used their popularity with the stock company as publicity. Sidney did not possess either the contacts or business savvy Laura had acquired from Pete. Now the roles were reversed; she took the lead. In their first program they sang three solos each and four duets, plus excerpts from various operas. The show was well received. The couple married in Baltimore and moved to Indianapolis.[128]

According to Bowman, "Indianapolis was rather a prejudiced town with disadvantages for colored performers. Although it was Sidney's home and everyone knew his family, we billed ourselves as a modern Hawaiian Duet and got by with it. We often played in theatres that did not allow colored patrons or performers."[129]

In 1923 Bowman and Kirkpatrick returned to New York City as members of the Ethiopian Art Players. Originally the Colored Folk Theatre, this Chicago-based group was organized in 1923 by Mrs. Sherwood Anderson and Raymond O'Neil.[130] The company's objective was to produce plays that dealt with Black life, but because of a lack of suitable material they presented mostly non-racial works.[131] Of the three plays presented, only one, *The Chip Woman's Fortune,* by Willis Richardson, was written by a Black playwright. In addition to *Chip Woman,* they performed Oscar Wilde's *Salomé* and a jazz version of Shakespeare's *The Comedy of Errors.* The Ethiopian Art Players, directed by O'Neil, first performed their three-play repertoire at the Lafayette Theatre in Harlem. However, when the community was unkind to the troupe, the producers moved them to Broadway in May 1923.[132]

On 7 May 1923 the company opened with *The Chip Woman's For-*

7. Laura and Sidney Kirkpatrick (c. 1916).

tune, followed by *Salomé,* at the Frazee Theatre in New York for eight performances. On 15 May 1923 the curtain raiser was *Chip Woman,* followed by *The Comedy of Errors* for seven performances, also at the Frazee.[133]

In *Salomé,* Kirkpatrick played Herod opposite Bowman's Herodias. According to a review in the *New York Times, Salomé* "is not particularly good and it is not particularly bad and it has its moments when it is art and other moments when it is theatre and still other moments when it is neither. Rather strangely for an Ethiopian Art Theatre, it seemed to one observer last night, it had no moments at all when it was Ethiopian."[134]

Chip Woman tells the story of an elderly Black woman, Aunt Nancy, who earns a living by collecting and selling chips of coal found in the streets. By living a very meager existence, she manages to save a large sum of money (which she hides in the backyard) for her son when he is released from prison. Bowman played Aunt Nancy. Even though it is never cited in the review, this landmark production was the first *drama* by a Black author to reach Broadway. The reporter from the *Times* did not mention Bowman; however, Percy Hammond, reviewing for the *Herald-Tribune,* wrote: "Miss Laura Bowman, as the cross Herodias, showed a gift of impersonation as an ancient negress in the curtain-raiser [*Chip Woman*] which preceded '*Salomé.*' "[135]

Bowman played Aemili in *The Comedy of Errors.* According to John Corbin, reviewing for the *New York Times, The Comedy of Errors* lacked the smoothness and precision of *Chip Woman* and *Salomé.* He went on to say:

Unlikely as it may appear, the director of the Ethiopian Art Theatre had an idea in the back of his head when he set out to jazz 'The Comedy of Errors'. . . . Raymond O'Neil pitches a circus tent, with a platform in the centre, in the manner of Jacques Copeau. Rude set pieces indicating the various scenes are fox-trotted in and shimmied out, to ragtime tunes, by black-face pierrots. Minor characters mime extravagantly to enliven the scene. . . . In brief the idea is to stage this Greco-Roman-Shakespearean farce in a gale of high spirits. . . . Instead of heightening the illusion, the attempted grotesqueries creaked at the hinges. It is quite possible that there is already a sufficient melange, what with Menander, Plautus and Shakespeare, without adding complexions of the various shades of cafe du lait and dissonances suggestive of the African jungle.[136]

Bowman and Kirkpatrick returned to Indianapolis where they worked in the surrounding area. Sometime later, when a new cast of the Lafayette Players opened at the Avenue Theatre in Chicago, Robert Levy, the boss from New York, asked Laura and Sidney to join. It appears that either the management had changed its policy regarding married couples or Bowman and Kirkpatrick were so popular that they were exempted. The couple signed a one-year contract with the Lafayette Players and returned to New York from which they were sent throughout the country.[137]

On 6 February 1928 *Meek Mose* opened at the Princess Theatre in New York for thirty-two performances.[138] Written by actor Frank Wilson (who had played the title role in *Porgy*), the play is set in Mexia, Texas, where a colony of Blacks has been evicted by greedy Whites. They find refuge in swamp country. Mose, the pacifist, believes in the expression "Blessed are the meek." After numerous sorrows, he triumphs in the end.[139] Bowman played Josephine, Mose's wife. Sidney was also in the cast.[140]

Produced by Lester Walton, the Black entrepreneur and newspaper man from the Lafayette, *Meek Mose* was the initial attempt at establishing the Princess Theatre in New York City as a Negro repertory theatre. In hopes of helping this idea to flourish, Mayor Walker, Otto H. Kuhn, Max Reinhardt, and other prominent political and theatre people attended the opening night performance. The *New York Times* provided the following review:

> it is difficult to record "Meek Mose" as anything better than a childishly naive endeavor, full of sepia tint John Golden and depicting life only in slightly shop-worn terms of the theatre. . . .
>
> On the other hand, the point may well be brought up that "Meek Mose" is not supposed to be a realistic portrayal of negroes or of contemporary negro problems, but simply a theatrical entertainment. In this case the opinion that such a theatre should locate in Harlem, where it would be of most service, might be in order.[141]

According to an article in the *Afro-American*, *Meek Mose* "ran the gamut of criticism which ranged from the 'feeble and faltering attempt' to a 'fruitful study of a man who took the Bible literally and tried to live by its creed.' "[142] The reporter cited examples from various critics. He quoted Alexander Wolcott of the *New York World:* " 'Mr. Wilson's play seemed to me an awkward and artless contraption and except for the excellent work of Laura Bowman as the mother, the company was not a promising one. . . . The redeeming feature of the production was the fact that when in doubt, 'Meek Mose' burst into the singing of spirituals, the players taking to them with the alacrity born of their knowledge that here was something they could do better than any one else.' "[143]

The *Afro-American* wrote, "Romeo Dougherty, of the *Amsterdam News* credited Laura Bowman, Ruth Ellis, and J. Lawrence Criner with portraying their roles faithfully." Despite praising the acting, Dougherty had this to say about the play: "The story, however, lacks sufficient depth we think to bring us to the theatre for the second time. We hope that it will have a liberal run, but we doubt it. It is, however, a very important step in the right direction." The *Brooklyn Eagle* said: "Wilson must be given credit for combining many elements of popular appeal in his first drama, including mob scenes and double weeding. One of the best parts is that of Laura Bowman, Mose's unbelieving wife."[144]

In 1928 Bowman organized a group of aspiring actors and began teaching dramatics. Known as the National Art School, located at 119th Street and Seventh Avenue in Harlem, her troupe performed at churches, schools, and social functions. Their repertoire included *The Unlighted Cross, The Passing of the Third Door Back,* and Oscar Wilde's *Salomé*. Pauline Meyers (Myers), Helen Mair, and Estelle Hemsley were among the members. From this time to the 1940s, Bowman had some kind of dramatic school.[145]

The fame of the Lafayette Players had spread to the West Coast years earlier. Prompted by repeated requests from the patrons for dramatic shows, the management of the Lincoln Theatre in Los Angeles invited the celebrated company to perform there. Located at Central Avenue and Twenty-third Street, the Lincoln became the home of the Lafayette Players for forty-two weeks. The group promised to present a varied program with a new type of dramatic performance each week. During this time, the company presented both old and new favorites.[146]

On 24 August 1928 the Lafayette Players premiered at the Lincoln Theatre in *Rain*. Lavishly produced, *Rain* was well received. Bowman and Kirkpatrick were in the company. According to Romeo Dougherty, writing this time for the *Pittsburgh Courier:* "The opening performance found the house sold out and many of the motion picture celebrities were on hand; in fact, Hollywood turned out in full and went away awed and surprised at the wonderful work of the colored artists."[147]

Rain, a favorite with New York audiences, gave Black theatregoers on the West Coast a "chance to view that which they had heard so much about," noted Thompson. "White critics were given a first-time opportunity to see black performers in serious drama."[148] The *Los Angeles American,* a White newspaper, was quoted by the *Amsterdam News:*

Painting in with broad strokes of comedy only hinted at in the
Caucasian productions of the melodrama, this interesting group
of Players presented an exciting mounting of the story which gave
Sadie Thompson a place in the bright annals of American drama.
Evelyn Preer, playing the vivid femme ... does commendatory
thespianism. ... A standing room only audience, which included
Charles Chaplin, and other Hollywood personalities cheered the
offering. The Lincoln production ... I regard as one of the most
interesting stage items of the current calendar.[149]

In the same article, "Los Angeles Gives Lafayette Players Remarkable Welcome at the Lincoln," the *Amsterdam News* quoted another
White newspaper, the *Los Angeles Illustrated Daily:*

With Jeanne Eagles appearing ... at the Orpheum this week, it is
a nice gesture on the part of the Lafayette Players to present *Rain*
as the opening attraction at the Lincoln Theatre. Four types of
actresses have played the dynamic and colorful role of Sadie
Thompson in the last two years. ... Each has had a distinct version ... so no odious comparison can be made. However, Evelyn
Preer, beautiful Negress, owes no apology to anyone for her interpretation. ... This group of Players, at the midnight show Saturday simply packed ... the beautiful Lincoln Theatre. ...[150]

After *Rain,* the company presented Willard Mack's drama *Kick In,*
followed by *In Old Kentucky.* During October they presented *Madame
X* as a "special attraction" for the Lincoln Theatre's first-year anniver-
sary. A few of the productions performed by the Lafayette Players dur-
ing the Fall of 1928 were: Bayard Veiller's *Within the Law; Anna
Christie* by Eugene O'Neill; *Is Zat So?* by James Gleason; *On Trial* by
Elmer Rice; *The Thirteenth Chair,* also by Veiller; Willard Mack's *The
Noose; Common Clay* by Cleve Kinkead; *Bought and Paid For* by
George Broadhurst; and Max Marcin's *Cheating Cheaters.* In Decem-
ber the Lafayette Players presented their first musical, Laurence
Schwab and B. G. de Sylva's *Queen High.* The show was a "triumphant
success." The players ended 1928 as the "undisputed hit of the sea-
son."[151]

The Lafayette Players opened 1929 with Ralph Spence's mystery
play *The Gorilla. Why Women Cheat, The Man Who Came Back* by
Jules Eckert Goodman, and Harlan Thompson's musical comedy *Little
Jesse James* were mounted during the remaining week of January. The
popular *Rain* was repeated during the first week of February, followed
by *Salomé.* Other shows produced during February and March were

John Emerson and Anita Loos's *The Whole Town's Talking; The Unborn* by Beulah Poytner; James Montgomery's musical comedy *Irene, the Fallen Sister;* and Michael Morton's play about the persecution of Jews, *The Yellow Ticket. Outcast* by Hubert Henry Davies ended the month of March. *Divorce, Dr. Jekyll and Mr. Hyde,* and (in honor of "Shriners' Week") *Are You a Mason?* were among the plays presented during April and May. During the last week of May, before the close of the season the Lafayette Players revived *The Unborn.*[152]

During her vacation, Bowman returned to New York. On 20 and 21 June 1929, she appeared in Jeroline Hemsley's *Wade in de Water* at the Abyssinia Baptist Church in Harlem. Under the patronage of Congressman Adam Clayton Powell, *Wade in de Water* was the debut production of the newly formed Negro Art Theatre.[153] (The price of tickets was 50¢.) Bowman was in the cast, presumably in the role Inez Clough would create at the Cherry Lane Theatre in September 1929. Pauline Meyers (Myers), one of Bowman's drama students, was also in the company. As with the Cherry Lane production, Hemsley Winfield played a featured part.[154]

While Bowman was in New York Evelyn Preer, after two weeks' vacation, returned to the Lafayette Players to star in Octavius Ray Cohen's *Come Seven.* The production was presented at the Orange Grove Theatre on Grand Street near Seventh Avenue in Los Angeles. *Come Seven* played for five consecutive weeks, closing during the latter part of August. Near the end of the run, attendance declined. During this time, Levy announced that the Players would be leaving Los Angeles for a limited engagement in San Francisco. On 15 September 1929 the Lafayette Players opened in the highly praised *Rain* at the Capitol Theatre in San Francisco.[155]

Perhaps in hopes of drumming up business, at the end of Summer, before going to San Francisco, Levy announced that the "New Lafayette Players" would be arriving in Los Angeles from New York to open the Fall season at the Lincoln Theatre. On 23 September 1929, the group opened with George V. Hobart's *Experience.* Abbie Mitchell, one of the "new" performers from New York, starred in the show. Also, Laura Bowman returned to the Lincoln for the Fall season. In October they presented the musical comedy *Hit the Deck,* an adaptation of Herbert Field's *Shore Leave.* They continued to present weekly productions throughout December. For Christmas week they staged Robert H. McLaughlin's *The Eternal Magdalene.* By this time, attendance had dropped so badly that the group's demise was inevitable. During January 1930, the Players staged their farewell performance, *Why Wives Go Wrong,* by an unknown playwright. The Lincoln Theatre closed; the venue would be reopened, however, as a movie theatre. Sometime later it was learned that Levy, the owner of the Lafayette Players, owed the company two weeks' salary, which they never received.[156] After the Lafayette Players disbanded, Bowman and Kirkpatrick remained in Los Angeles. They became members of the Hall Singers, obtained a contract from R.K.O., and sang in several films including *Dixie Anna* with Bebe Daniels, *Check and Double Check* with Amos and Andy, and *Half Shot at Sunrise.*[157]

Bowman returned to the East Coast where on 25 December 1931 she appeared in Lula Vollmer's *Sentinels* at the Biltmore Theatre in New York for eleven performances.[158] Set in the South, *Sentinels* tells the story of the Hathaways, a wealthy White family, whose son kills a local scoundrel. When Mallie, the Black mammy who has raised the Hathaway boys as her own, discovers that George has committed the murder, in order to save the family name she forces her own son, Thunder, to take the blame. At the end of the play, however, as Thunder is being taken away by the law, George confesses. Laura Bowman portrayed Mallie, the family servant; Wayland Rudd was Thunder.[159]

Virtually all of the critics panned the play but cited Bowman as giving an excellent performance. Brooks Atkinson of the *New York Times* said: "*Sentinels* is an awkward and labored piece of writing for the stage, elaborately motivated in the early scenes to assure the heroics of the concluding act. In spite of two or three isolated examples of good acting, the performance as a whole is quite ambiguous. . . . Laura Bowman makes something warm of the monotonously written part of the Negro servant."[160] Richard Lockridge in the New York *Sun* wrote, "It is always overburdened with incidental characters, well enough conceived and better acted, but not in themselves sturdy enough – or novel enough – to make *Sentinels* a play. . . . Particularly good are Miss Bowman and Mr. Rudd, both Negroes."[161]

Burns Mantle, reviewing for the *New York News,* credited Bowman and Rudd with saving the play:

> Laura Bowman, late leading woman of the Harlem stock company, and Wayland Rudd, hailing from the same training school, arose in the third act and played a big scene so earnestly that they momentarily brought reality to a slightly synthetic theatre piece and helped the evening tremendously. . . .
>
> Playing it fervently and yet simply, Miss Bowman and Mr. Rudd were able to win an applausive tribute from their audience. . . . the evening, histrionically, belongs to the Harlem players. . . .[162]

Four months later Bowman was back on Broadway. On 12 April 1932 Richard Mailbaum's *The Tree* opened at the Park Lane Theatre (formerly Daly's Sixty-Third Street Theatre) for seven performances.[163] *The Tree* takes place in a rural district North of the Mason-Dixon line. David, a friendly Black youth, is caught dancing for a White girl under a tree. Later, she is found raped and murdered. The Black youth is erroneously accused and hanged. After the real killer (who happens to be White) is discovered, in order to make amends one of the White lynchers allows himself to be hanged with the same rope under the same tree. Laura Bowman played Miriam, the mother of the slain Black youth.[164]

This drama of lynching in the North did not fare well with the critics. Bowman's performance, however, was praised. The New York *Amsterdam News* called *The Tree* a "Morbid Drama." It went on to say: "The most heart-throbbing and emotional performance of the evening was given by Laura Bowman, as Miriam, David's mother."[165] The *Chicago Defender* reported: "The scene in which Laura Bowman, as Miriam, David's mother, rocks the dead body of her son to sleep and sings to her Jesus has genuine, throat-choking tears of compassion."[166] John Mason Brown, reviewing for *The Post*, said: "Laura Bowman had a chance as the slain Negro's mammy to croon woeful songs once again over a colored son to whom the whites had done a wrong. Good as some of Mr. Rossen's [the director] actors were, however, Mr. Mailbaum's solemn drama was far from being good enough. It was, to tell the truth, rather sad in more ways than one."[167]

Brooks Atkinson did not mention Bowman by name. He did, however, note her performance: "Although the acting is clumsy and faltering, the mob scenes have a genuine clamor, and the scene in which the Negro's mother wearily rocks his dead body to sleep and sings to her Jesus has an honest sense of compassion." He added, "the author and most of the actors still have a good deal to learn about the theatre."[168]

After years of performing in musicals, vaudeville, and with the Lafayette Players, Bowman had begun establishing herself as a dramatic actress on the professional legitimate stage. Although the shows were short-lived and Bowman's roles were stereotyped, she had two Broadway openings within six months: *Sentinels* and *The Tree*. "That, at that time, was considered quite an achievement," she said.[169]

For some time, Levy and a group of former Lafayette Players (including Bowman) had been attempting to re-establish the troupe at the Lincoln Theatre. It was announced that the Players would reopen in June and that Jules Wolf, the new manager of the Lincoln, had sent for Laura Bowman to come to Los Angeles from Boston to join the company. During the week of 25 June 1932 the Lafayette Players opened at the Lincoln (no production information found). During the week of July 4th they presented O'Neill's *Desire under the Elms.* The group's revival, however, was short-lived. On Sunday, 17 July 1932, the Lafayette Players gave their last performance at the Lincoln Theatre, before disbanding permanently. Ironically, the title of the feature film that opened at the Lincoln the following Sunday was the "all-colored" *Harlem Is Heaven.*[170] "For so many fruitful and productive years," observed Thompson, "Harlem had been almost that for the Lafayette Players."[171]

Bowman remained in Los Angeles for several months after the demise of the Lafayette Players. During this time she debuted on the screen in *Ten Minutes to Live* (1932) produced by Oscar Micheaux. In 1933 she made the film *Drums of Voodoo,* produced by Robert Mintz and Louis Weiss.[172] Soon afterward the couple bought a car and Sidney drove back to the East Coast. Shortly after their return, they performed their duo at the Alhambra Theatre at Seventh Avenue and Twelfth Street in New York City. A few days later, Sidney died in Harlem Hospital of a heart attack.[173]

Once again Bowman was left a widow. Nonetheless, she continued to earn a living as a serious actress. A few weeks later, on 20 February 1933, J. Augustus Smith's *Louisiana* opened at the Majestic Theatre in Brooklyn, New York, for one week of performances. Set in the Louisiana swamps, this three-act drama with a prologue depicts the conflict between voodoo and Christianity. J. Augustus Smith played Amos Berry, the preacher; Bowman was Aunt Hagar, the voodoo priestess.[174]

According to the reviewer for the *Brooklyn Daily Eagle:* "In a way it is a more truthful picture of colored religious life than *Green Pastures.* It cannot be as popular with a white audience as the latter play, for *Green Pastures* flattered the vanity of whites by allowing them to laugh at what they thought was a colored man's idea of God and the Bible." Despite reporting that the play "is poorly written" and "sadly in need of a good director," he went on to say: "But the last act, with its darkened stage, its drums continually beating, its voodoo witch – if witch is the right name for old Aunt Hagar – its blind villain and its weird singing and dancing is the most unusual and dramatic scene of the play." Of the individual performances, he said: "Laura Bowman, who plays Aunt Hagar, is the domineering figure. Here is a role that plays itself but Miss Bowman adds a good deal to it."[175]

One week later, on 27 February 1933, *Louisiana* moved uptown to the Forty-eighth Street Theatre for eight performances.[176] For the most part, the reviews were unfavorable. Bowman's performance, however, was praised. Burns Mantle, the critic for the New York *Daily News,* wrote the most favorable review:

The play is an unpretentious exhibit of primitive drama punctu-
ated by the occasional singing of spirituals. In one or two scenes,
notably a church scene in which the honest pastor is forced by his
enemy to confess a murder done thirty years before, it rises
sharply to climaxes of emotional power.

An outstanding performance in the all-colored cast is that of
Laura Bowman as Aunt Hagar. An ominous, brooding exultant
figure of vengeance, she dominated all her scenes. . . .[177]

Shortly after Sidney Kirkpatrick's death, Laura began to drink at
home alone (after work) in order to sleep. Soon she was drinking heavily
at a local bar in Harlem that theatre people frequented. While there,
she met her fourth husband-to-be, LeRoi Antoine. Antoine, a Haitian
who had aspirations of becoming an opera singer, was twenty-three
years her junior. She called him "my boy," and many of her friends
called her a "cradle snatcher." With the exception of Anita Bush, the
old-timers objected to the relationship. Despite this, she became Antoine's benefactor.[178] "I planned all sorts of things for his entertainment
or amusement," recalled Bowman. "I never invited people unless they
were musical or celebrities. I kept him in touch with the best people at
all times."[179] Bowman had become accustomed to being loved by the
men with whom she was involved. Antoine, however, did not care for
her as a lover; "I never think of you as a sweetheart, but sometimes, I
wish, oh, how I wish that you were my mother," he revealed to her.[180]

A short time after meeting, Bowman and Antoine were married. For
seven years she taught him everything she knew about music and singing. She paid for voice lessons from Prof. Franz Erdody, a prominent
teacher at the time. When Antoine was ready, she gave him a recital at
the Steinway Recital Hall on Fifty-seventh Street in New York City.
Bowman's protégé received creditable reviews from the *New York
Times* and *The Mirror.*[181]

By the end of 1933 Bowman was back on Broadway in Owen Davis's
Jezebel. On 19 December 1933 *Jezebel* opened at the Ethel Barrymore
Theatre for thirty-two performances.[182] This three-act play with songs
and spirituals takes place in the antebellum South. A Southern belle
returns three years after quarreling with her lover to find him married.
She instigates a duel in which her ex-lover's brother kills the opponent.
She is branded a Jezebel by her aunt and is blamed for the murder.
When her ex-lover is stricken with yellow fever, she goes to nurse him
on the plague-ridden island from which neither of them returns.[183]

The title role, Jezebel, performed by film star Miriam Hopkins, was
originally written for Tallulah Bankhead. Due to illness, however, she
was unable to play the part. Laura Bowman played Mammy Winnie.

Dido Johnson, reviewing for the *Daily Citizen* (city unknown), wrote: "In *Jezebel* Miss Bowman gives one of her finest characterizations, that of the Negro woman whose love for the hellion who was her mistress (Miriam Hopkins) passed all understanding."[184] Bushnell Dimond, of the *Columbus Journal Dispatch,* said: "I like immensely . . . all the Negroes, especially Laura Bowman as a pacific mammy. . . ."[185] Brooks Atkinson summed up the general feeling of the critics: "Reed Brown Jr. is excellent as the lover. As the aunt Cora Witherspoon is in top form. Frederic Worlock as the general has the convictions of a Southern gentleman and the breeding of a good actor. There are good performances also by Owen Davis Jr., Helen Claire, Frances Creel of the California Creels and Laura Bowman. But Mr. Davis's romantic play of the Southland is only a Bowery trollop at heart."[186]

By January 1934 *Drums of Voodoo* was being shown in the movie theatres. *Drums of Voodoo* was the film version of Augustus Smith's play *Louisiana.* The original stage players re-created the roles they had performed on Broadway. Bowman was Aunt Hagar. *Drums of Voodoo* is "the most powerful drama of jungle superstition ever to be brought to the screen," raved the *Washington Tribune.* "You will love Aunt Hagar, despite the fact that she practices voodooism. Underneath her exterior of witchcraft there is a heart of love for humanity."[187]

On October 1934, Henry Rosendahl's *Yesterday's Orchid* opened at the Fulton Theatre (in Brooklyn, New York) for three performances.[188] The play is about a girl who manages to get a lot of money from several men while remaining virtuous.[189] Bowman was Caroline. That *Yesterday's Orchid* closed after only three performances is indicative of the reactions of the press. Kauf, from *Variety,* reported: "Nothing in the playwriting, the acting or the production to commend it."[190] According to Richard Lockridge of the New York *Sun,* "The acting of Carlton Young and Miss Whitney is not quite so bad as that of Royal Stout, Laura Bowman, Kay Linaker, William Balfour, Grant Erwin, Charles Dingle and Richard Reeves."[191]

Like Inez Clough, Bowman was heard on NBC's Sunday afternoon radio program of plays of "life among colored folk." Bowman appeared in F. Carlton Moss's *Careless Love.* She was paid $55 per broadcast. During the Thirties, radio became quite profitable for Bowman. She played eighteen weeks with Helen Hayes on the *New Penny Show.* Bowman earned $125 for one night a week, plus $100 for rebroadcasting on the weekends. She was performing on four or five radio programs, as well as soap operas for Procter and Gamble. Bowman's radio credits included *Stella Dallas, John's Other Wife, Pepper Young's Family, The O'Neils,* and *Pretty Kitty Kelly. Personal Column on the Air* was another radio show on which Bowman was heard. On Sunday mornings Bowman was heard on the *Southernaires;* on Sunday evenings she was heard on *Pores and Drums.*[192] "In fact, there was not a single day that I did not broadcast on some program," said Bowman.[193] In 1935 she was seen in Oscar Micheaux's *Lem Hawkin's Confession.*[194]

On 26 October 1936 Sophie Treadwell's *Plumes in the Dust* previewed out of town at the National Theatre in Washington, D.C. This three-act sketch of the life of Edgar Allan Poe was produced and staged by Arthur Hopkins, with Henry Hull as Poe. Laura Bowman was Miranda, presumably the maid/housekeeper. Pauline Myers, Bowman's acting student, played Lou. "Its characters, other than Poe, are unconvincing; its lines, except for those borrowed from Poe are flat," wrote one reviewer.[195] A few days later, on 6 November 1936, *Plumes in the Dust* opened at the 46th Street Theatre in New York for eleven performances.[196] The New York press was more supportive than the Washington critics were.

In 1937 Bowman and Antoine went to Haiti to visit his family for several months. While they were there, Antoine collected Haitian music and folklore. When they returned to New York, the Negro Unit of WPA's Federal Theatre was presenting William Du Bois's *Haiti.*[197] *Haiti* opened on 2 March 1938 at the Lafayette Theatre in Harlem for 168 performances.[198] It told the story of the uprising, led by Henri Christophe and Toussaint L'Ouverture, against the French.[199]

After the opening of the play, it was discovered that there was no background music. When it was learned that Antoine had brought back some music from Haiti, he and Bowman were asked to help with the music. They were both placed on salary so *Haiti* could use their songs. After witnessing the christening of the authentic Haitian virgin drums played in the performance, Walter Damrosch asked Antoine to appear on an international hookup to broadcast these songs. According to Bowman, "this was the actual introduction of Haitian folklore and music to the American public and the world."[200]

On 31 October 1938 Waller Freeman's *Conjur* opened at the St. Felix Playhouse in Brooklyn. *Conjur* is the story of a young Black girl who is in love with a son of a Conjur woman. When a minister comes into her life, she is forced to deal with the struggle to banish conjur superstitions in favor of religion. Bowman played Parthenia, the Conjur woman. Ida Forsyne was a member of the congregation. According to the New York *Post,* "If there were prizes to be given one would go to Laura Bowman who plays Parthenia, the Conjur woman. . . ."[201]

Conjur was a landmark production. As Brooks Atkinson pointed out: "According to a mimeographed bulletin handed out to the visiting drama soothsayers, 'the very thought of the Brattleboro Theatre presenting a new play with an all-Negro cast was in itself somewhat revo-

8. Laura Bowman as Parthenia, the Conjur woman in *Conjur* (1938). Photo courtesy of The Billy Rose Theatre Collection, The New York Public Library for the Performing Arts, Astor, Lenox and Tilden Foundations.

lutionary in Brooklyn circles.' "[202] Except for Atkinson, most of the critics agreed that the play was well cast and well acted. Atkinson had this to say:

> Although parts of it are well written with some literary skill, it is virtually undramatic in story, acting and staging. The Juanita Hall Choir sings the customary spirituals during the familiar church meeting scene. . . . The Brattleboro Theatre might arouse warmer interest in its future if it worked through a nucleus of ambitious actors. Without an acting company it is only a producing unit; that puts it in competition with Broadway, which is already much more skillful in the business of producing than a small organization can hope to be.[203]

Also in 1938, Bowman was seen on the screen in Oscar Micheaux's *God's Stepchildren*.[204]

On 16 March 1939 Mary McCarthy's *Please Mrs. Garibaldi* opened at the Belmont Theatre in New York for four performances.[205] A variation of *My Darling Daughter*, this "American comedy" deals with an Italian-American family living in San Francisco.[206] A daughter has made one mistake. In the end, however, with the help of her loving parents, the girl happily marries the young man.[207] Laura Bowman played Endora, presumably the maid. (Black female servants were rarely given last names.) Perhaps, the fact that the show only ran for four performances is indicative of the critics' reactions. "What happened on the stage of the Belmont Theatre last night was nothing less than a Turkey," said the *New York Daily News*.[208] "Play has no sparkle, few laughs and not enough acting," wrote *Variety*.[209]

Because of his success with *Haiti*, Antoine became recognized as the leading authority on Haitian folklore and music. Warner Brothers produced a film in New York, *Voodoo Fire*, starring Floyd Gibbons; Antoine co-starred. When he decided to pursue a film career, he and Bowman moved to Los Angeles.[210] "What we didn't know was that Hollywood was and still is the most disappointing prospect in show business. I found that all my previous experience was wasted and did not count," said Bowman.[211]

Fortunately she still had a film contract. In 1940 Bowman appeared as Dr. Helen Jackson, the leading role, in *Son of Ingagi*, produced by R. Kahn, an independent studio.[212] Written by Spencer Williams, *Son of Ingagi* is significant as the first all-Black horror film.[213] Also in 1940, Bowman was seen in *The Notorious Elinor Lee*. Produced by Hubert Julian and Oscar Micheaux, "Robert Earl Jones [James Earl Jones's father] plays a fighter on the rise and Edna Mae Harris, the woman who tried to stop him by using her wiles and getting him to 'throw' the fight."[214] The studio was able to get Bowman accepted into the Screen Actors Guild. Antoine, however, could not get into the union, and without a Guild card, he could not get a job. Although he was not pleased with the role, he was eventually cast as a primitive drummer in *Rhapsody in Blue*. In addition to roles in *Sundown* and *Belle of Yukon*, Antoine was hired as technical director for *Lydia Bailey*, a film about Haiti produced by Twentieth-Century Fox.[215]

The couple remained in California where Bowman organized an amateur theatre group. "I soon discovered that people were not too theatre-minded," she said.[216] Eventually Bowman met a woman who was directing a radio program for the Gold Furniture Company. She invited Bowman and her troupe to present a Monday night dramatic program. Lacking money for original radio scripts, they performed excerpts from old stock plays and Bible stories. The program became so popular that Bowman was asked by Rev. Clayton Russell of the Independent Church to perform regularly scheduled programs in the church auditorium. They produced plays such as *The Rosary, The Passing of the Third Door Back,* and *The Eternal Magdalene*. Soon Bowman and her group were being invited to other churches to perform. These opportunities provided valuable experience for Bowman's students. "This was not very remunerative to me, but it kept me active," said Bowman.[217]

Bowman heard of a small theatre group, headed by Paul Bernard at the Vanguard Theatre located at Hollywood Boulevard and La Brea, that was presenting *Decision*. *Decision* had been produced on Broadway in 1944. One of the roles required a "Negro dialect"; Bowman played the part. During the run of the show, Bowman was seen by many directors, producers, and writers. This led to Robert Ardrey writing a part for her in his play *Jeb,* starring Ossie Davis. Bowman signed a contract for $250 a week and transportation to New York where she began rehearsals for *Jeb.*[218]

Jeb, a postwar drama, tells the story of a World War II Black veteran who returns to the South. Although he has won a Silver Star and a Purple Heart, he is denied a "White" job running the adding machine as a clerk in a mill. A conflict occurs, and Jeb flees to the North.[219] Before entering the war, Davis had performed in *On Striver's Row* and *Joy Exceeding Glory* with the semi-professional Rose McClendon Players.[220] With his appearance as Jeb, however, Davis debuted on the professional stage. Laura Bowman played Amanda Turner, Jeb's mother, and Ruby Dee portrayed his girlfriend. While *Jeb* was rehearsing at the Amsterdam Roof Theatre, Bowman roomed in the Bronx with Susie Sutton.[221]

On 7 February 1946, *Jeb* previewed at the Locust Street Theatre in

9. Cinema flier for *Son of Ingagi* (1940). This was the first all-black horror film. Photo courtesy of Hatch-Billops Collection.

Philadelphia for ten days. According to *Variety,* "Ossie Davis, a practical unknown, himself just out of service after four years in uniform with the Army Medical Corps, does a crackerjack job as Jeb. . . . Laura Bowman is outstanding as his mother, and Ruby Dee as his sweetheart does exceptionally well with one of the play's most difficult roles. . . ."[222] Ossie Davis's and Ruby Dee's stage romance blossomed into a real-life romance and eventually they were married.

On 21 February 1946, three weeks after previewing in Philadelphia, *Jeb* opened on Broadway at the Martin Beck Theatre and ran for only nine performances.[223] The *New York Times* cited Ossie Davis as giving the best performance. Despite commending the directing, acting, and setting, Lewis Nichols found *Jeb* lacking as drama. "For it Mr. Ardrey has written several moving and stirring scenes, which Mr. Shumlin has directed and the actors perform with the highest artistry of the theatre. But, on strictly dramatic terms, *Jeb* is not all of a piece. . . . The suggestion for a great and stirring play is there, but it is not realized."[224]

In an unidentified article, "Goodbye to a Good Play," Irene Kittle Kamp disagreed with Nichols on most points:

> *Jeb* was a better, more honest, less complicated treatment of the Negro's problem than *Deep Are the Roots.* If it has its faults they are not big enough to rob it of its enormous drama. . . .
>
> The production and the acting (except for Ossie Davis in the title role and Santos Ortega as a white liberal) seemed terribly stylized and Mielziner's sets an unhappy attempt to symbolize rather than represent. . . .
>
> For me, the play ended with a terrible scene behind the white church into which Jeb has gone believing that the good people of the town, if faced with the truth, will be . . . good. With that scene Mr. Ardrey handed me and, I'm sure, most sensitive white people, a very hot potato. I did not find it possible to throw the potato in the aisle when the curtain fell. I think this makes *Jeb* a good play.[225]

"The show *Jeb* was an interesting one to play, but the short run was none too pleasant," recalled Bowman. "No sooner had we recovered from the excitement of opening night than everybody began to discuss the closing."[226]

Immediately following the opening of *Jeb,* Bowman, Ossie Davis, and Ruby Dee were contacted by John Wildberg, its producer, to perform in one of the touring companies of *Anna Lucasta* (1944).[227] Originally performed in 1944 by the American Negro Theatre at the 135th

Street Library in Harlem, Abram Hill's adaptation of Philip Yordan's play about a Polish family became a Broadway hit.[228] *Anna Lucasta* was so successful that it played at the Manfield Theatre for 957 performances.[229] Bowman, who played Theresa, the role created by Georgia Burke on Broadway, did not go to Europe with the Broadway cast; she performed on the subway circuit. This tour included the Bronx, Brooklyn, Atlantic City, and other outlying areas. "The company transferred our baggage from one theatre to the other, and most of the time we could get to the theatres by subway," said Bowman.[230]

A few months later, the circuit was divided. Bowman played two weeks each in Detroit, Providence, and Massachusetts. "Each trip was greater in success, and, when we got close to New York, I also played with the New York cast, taking advantage of the contract I had," said Bowman. Georgette Harvey and Alberta Perkins had already played the part. Despite opening on Broadway again for the second time in one season, Bowman was not entirely satisfied. "Anybody would have been pleased to work on Broadway, but not on the road salary," she revealed. She went back on the road with the show. After four years of touring *Anna Lucasta* finally closed in Canada. Bowman returned to Los Angeles.[231]

By this time Bowman weighed over 200 pounds. Around 1951, soon after she returned home, she suffered a paralyzing stroke that confined her to a wheelchair. Although he desired to become a classical singer, in order to support himself and Bowman, Antoine embarked on a nightclub singing career. For six years Antoine cared for Bowman singlehandedly. Unable to either walk or move her body without help, Bowman relied on Antoine completely. She was painfully aware of the stress her illness had placed on him. "Poor LeRoi. What would I do without him? Life has not been easy for this young man I married," lamented Bowman.[232] Although the Negro Actors Guild, of which Bowman was a charter member, and some of her church and theatre friends remembered her from time to time, Bowman credited Antoine with sustaining her: "As I look back through the years, I remember how many friends condemned this marriage because of the difference in our ages. They said I would be sorry. The wisest thing I ever did was to marry LeRoi Antoine. I know now that he will never leave me, and, as long as he is able, I will be cared for. These friends have long forgotten me."[233]

Confined to her bed during the twilight years of her life, Bowman would reminisce. "I owe all I ever learned about show business to Pete Hampton," she said.[234] Concerning show business, Bowman advised that "no one without education and special training make an attempt to start because there are too many heartaches when you don't succeed."[235] She credited choral director Bill Elkins and Madame DeHart, one of the original Fisk Jubilee singers from Fisk University, with providing her musical training.[236] "In dramatics I am thankful to Billy King, Hattie McIntosh, and the Lafayette Players," said Bowman. "The best training possible is in a stock company. It gives you a chance to become versatile."[237]

During her many years of performing, Bowman earned a considerable amount of money. Yet she was now broke. "In my early training I was not taught the value of money," she said. "Therefore, I have suffered from what others call extravagance, although it did not seem so at the time. . . . I am afraid that I have spent most of my money on myself, but I did buy many things for others."[238]

Bowman spent her entire adult life in show business. Her experiences, however, left her with bittersweet feelings: "I must say that my fifty years in the theatre have been most colorful. But I cannot encourage any of the young aspirants to try it because it is hard work and there is nothing sure. There are lots of disappointments. I am very grateful to my co-workers for their help and encouragement, but, nonetheless, I have paid a price for my fifty years."[239]

On 29 March 1957, at the age of seventy-six, Bowman died in Los Angeles. She was survived by her husband, LeRoi Antoine. According to the obituary, "Laura Bowman Is Dead," in the *New York Times:* "It was said of Miss Bowman that she had played in about every country that had a theatre."[240]

Like her counterparts Inez Clough, Lottie Grady, and Anita Bush, Bowman made a successful transition from musical theatre to become a respected character actress. Although the majority of her stage roles were as servants and she had to "blacken up" to play the parts, Bowman was more often than not singled out as having given an excellent performance. Through her association with the Lafayette Players, community theatre companies, and her own amateur acting groups, Bowman helped to foster the development of Black Theatre. That Laura Bowman not only survived but succeeded in an institution as unpredictable as show business is a testimony to her talent and determination.

As has been stated, on 5 July 1898 Will Marion Cook and Paul Laurence Dunbar's landmark musical *Clorindy; or The Origin of the Cakewalk* opened at the Casino Roof Garden in New York City. *Clorindy* was the first all-Black production to play in a major theatre patronized exclusively by Whites.[241] Abbie Mitchell first appeared on the professional stage in 1898, at the age of fourteen, when she took over the lead in *Clorindy* during its run in Chicago.[242]

Born of musical parents (an African-American mother and a German-Jewish father) in New York on 25 September 1884, Mitchell was educated in a convent in Baltimore.[243] After her mother's death, Mitchell was offered the option of living with her father's family where she could pass for White. Instead she chose to stay with Mama Alice, the Black woman who had been raising her, and live as a Black.[244] Mitchell began singing at local church affairs as a child. Early in her career, she was coached by Cook, whom she married the year after appearing in *Clorindy*, and she studied in New York with Harry T. Burleigh.[245]

She performed songs of Paul Laurence Dunbar's poems taught to her by her husband in a series of Sunday evening concerts on Broadway. She also sang at parties hosted by the Vanderbilts, Astors, and Morgans. In December 1898, Abbie Mitchell joined "Black Patti's Troubadours" and toured with the troupe off and on for several seasons. Throughout her life she admired Mme. Jones and spoke of her often. The summer following *Clorindy*, Mitchell was a principal in Cook's musical *Jes Lak White Folks* (1899) at the New York Winter Garden.[246]

By 1903 she was in London with Williams and Walker's *In Dahomey*. A principal, she was a hit playing Pansy and singing "Brownskin Baby Mine." Mitchell's popularity had been underestimated by both her husband and Williams and Walker. "For some reason the producers left Mitchell in the hotel, thinking she would not be missed. Noting her absence, the king, who had seen the show, asked: " 'Where's "She ain't no violet"?' " (That was the nickname Londoners had given her: the first line in the song by Will Marion Cook, "Brownskin Baby Mine," Mitchell's featured number.) The king sent his royal coach to fetch her before permitting the performance to go on."[247]

According to Mitchell's granddaughter, Maranantha Quick, a.k.a. Marion Douglas Quick, Mitchell told this anecdote often. Even as a teenager, Mitchell was strong-willed, determined, and precocious. When she discovered that the royal coach had come for her, she purposefully took her time dressing, keeping King Edward VII waiting. When she arrived at the palace, to her surprise, she found the king and Cook on their knees shooting craps.[248]

Mitchell's acceptance by the London audience had inspired her to develop her talent and become a serious singer. Her plans were to reach the top of her profession. When she returned to the United States, without her husband's knowledge, she pawned all of her jewelry (for which she received $2,000) and went to the nationally known Madame Emilia Seranno whom she begged to teach her until the money ran out. Even though Mitchell's actions were met by the dismay and disapproval of Cook, determined to get the training she felt she needed, she refused to redeem her jewelry.[249]

In 1904 Mitchell portrayed Mandy Lou, a principal in Cook's musical *The Southerners*. Ida Forsyne danced a solo and Laura Bowman was in the chorus. "While the *New York Dramatic Mirror* despised the musical of life on the old plantation, it raved about Mitchell: 'Miss Mitchell won her laurels by singing a quaint, wistful Negro song called 'Mandy Lou' in so sincere a fashion that for the moment the artificiality of the rest of the performance was forgotten and the audience was surprised into genuine feeling. The song was demanded again and again. The singer had actually touched the hearts of Broadway playgoers.' "[250]

In 1905, she was a member of the original Nashville Students, the first all-Black concert group. Composed of twenty entertainers who sang and played music written in the "Negro" style, they debuted in the Spring of 1905 at the Proctor 23rd Street Theatre in New York. Mitchell was the featured soprano and Ida Forsyne the featured dancer. They were so successful that they played at the Hammerstein Victoria Theatre on Broadway during the day and at the Casino Roof Garden at night. Later they toured Europe for eight months as the Memphis Students, playing at the Palace Theatre in London, the Olympia in Paris, and the Shumann Circus in Berlin.[251] Mitchell starred again in the second edition of the Memphis Students in 1908.[252] During this time, she studied voice with Jean de Reszke in Paris.[253]

Mitchell did not receive the support of her friends and colleagues when she decided to become a classical singer. They felt that she should have been satisfied singing popular music. When she gave her first concert in New York (no date found), Mitchell felt the hostility from certain members of the audience. According to her granddaughter, Mitchell was a fighter and she produced her best work when she was challenged. Her performance for the concert was highly praised. Mitchell, who was very dramatic in speech and behavior, ended the story by telling her granddaughter, "they came to laugh; they stayed to cheer."[254]

Also in 1908 Mitchell, one of the principals in Williams and Walker's last production, *Bandana Land,* sang "Red Red Rose." In addition to praising the two stars, a critic reviewing for the *Brooklyn Eagle* wrote: "There are half a dozen other good actors and singers in the company, including that wonderfully sympathetic soprano, Abbie Mitchell Cook."[255] She starred as the lead soprano Minnehaha (singing "Cupid is an Indian Pickininny") in Cole and Johnson's *The Red Moon* and in 1908 she toured Europe in the role where she sang a command performance for Czar Nicholas II of Russia.[256] Mitchell starred in Marion A. Brooks, Charles A. Hunter, James T. Brymn, and H. Lawrence Freeman's musical *Panama* in 1908 at the Pekin Stock Company in Chicago. The story deals with the problems encountered by the residents of Brandyville, Kentucky, when they are duped into investing in a mythical piece of property in Panama. The acts shift between the canal region of Panama and Kentucky.[257]

Mitchell also made a name for herself touring in vaudeville. In July 1909 she and Tom Fletcher starred in "The Lime Kiln Club" at the American Theatre in New York. The act, featuring performers from the Williams and Walker company, was based on the "end of the first act of 'Bandanna Land.'" Mitchell sang two songs, one in the opening of the act and one in the closing of the act. In the latter number she wore bluejean overalls and sang "Down among the Sugar Cane."[258] According to *Variety*, "with Miss Mitchell's agreeable soprano voice, backed by the massive male chorus offstage, the number is worked up in splendid shape. . . . The singing alone is enough to carry the act as far as it wants to go in vaudeville."[259]

In October 1909 Mitchell performed at the American Music Hall in Chicago, and "has the distinction of being the second black woman in America to play first-class houses in a single act and not buck dancing. The first was Rachel Walker, who played Hammerstein's Roof Garden, New York City, for four months without intermission."[260]

By March 1910 she was at the Wigwam in San Francisco. "A rich voice, splendid enunciation and finished acting ability 'suiting the action of the word,' as it were, are a combination that passes Miss Abbie Mitchell as one of the season's best in her line," reported *Variety*.[261] On 28 May 1910 Mitchell became the "first colored woman to do a single vaudeville turn at the Majestic Theatre, New York City."[262] In July of that year she appeared at the Pekin Theatre in Chicago. Songs in her act included "Cousin, Caruso," "As Long as the World Goes Round," and "Mammy's Little Molasses Candy Boy."[263]

When Mitchell's son Mercer was stricken with scarlet fever, she lost her voice as a result of nursing him back to health. Mitchell turned to the dramatic stage. Since she considered herself a singer, not an actress, the transition to drama was difficult for her.[264] During this time, however, she studied harmony and musical theory under Metville Charlton.[265] In 1916, when she first joined the Lafayette Players, the *Indianapolis Freeman* headlined: "Miss Abbie Mitchell, America's Acknowledged Great Singer, Now Appearing in Drama." Mitchell performed with the Lafayette Players at intervals up to 1929.[266]

In the spring of 1916 Mitchell was seen in *Paid in Full* and *Under Cover*. As one of the "new stars," she earned $90 a week. During the week of 18 September 1916 she appeared in her first leading role with the Lafayette Players in Alexander Brisson's *Madame X*. This was a role she would repeat many times.[267] According to the *Amsterdam News*, "she had minor parts for several months, learned overnight the part consisting of long speeches in 104 pages so successfully that she was handed the lead."[268]

The play ran for nearly three and a half hours, ending just before midnight. The packed house demanded numerous curtain calls and the critics were very supportive.[269] Lucien H. White of the *New York Age* felt that "the 'high-water' mark of their efforts had been attained in their presentation of *Madame X.* . . . His highest acclaim was for the star of the production, Miss Mitchell, whom he lavishly compared to Sarah Bernhardt who at the zenith of her own career also portrayed Madame X."[270]

In October, *Madame X* was presented in Baltimore and Washington. The play was so successful in Washington that it broke attendance records at the Howard Theatre.[271] Washington critic R. W. Thompson, reviewing for the *Indianapolis Freeman,* agreed with the critic from the *New York Age:* "Abbie Mitchell Caps Climax in *Madame X.* Miss Abbie Mitchell placed the cap-sheaf upon her brilliant career. She was a marvel and sustained the trying role with a force and finish that has not been surpassed by Sarah Bernhardt, Dorothy Donnely, Eugenie Blair or any of the great stars who have preceded her in this part."[272]

Mitchell went on to star in John Roberts's *The Conspiracy* and Goethe's *Faust* at the Howard Theatre. Directed by A. C. Winn, this presentation of *Faust* introduced six songs from the operatic version of the play, including "The Flower Song" and "The Jewel Song." Mitchell played the tragic Marguerite opposite Sidney Kirkpatrick's (Laura Bowman's future husband) Mephisto.[273]

After nine months of offering an assortment of dramas, melodramas, and comedies, the Lafayette Players presented their first full-length musical, George M. Cohan's popular *Forty-five Minutes from Broadway,* directed by A. C. Winn. For this show, a chorus of female dancers was added. The company now included thirty members, the largest cast for a single production. Having regained her singing voice, Abbie Mitchell played the leading role of Mary, the maid.[274] According to White: "Abbie Mitchell as Mary Jane Jenkins, the housemaid, is clever and capable, and her one song, 'Mary Is a Grand Old Name,' is sung as only Miss Mitchell can sing."[275]

The *Indianapolis Freeman* reported that "Cohan's play with music was filled with as much dramatic blending as could possibly have been put into a strictly musical comedy production."[276] One of the main attractions at the theatre was the Lafayette Ladies' Orchestra under the direction of Marie Lucas, Sam Lucas's daughter. They played before performances, during intermissions, and after last curtain calls. For *Forty-five Minutes from Broadway,* they "played 'as though inspired' " by the house-maid costumes they wore. As a special feature for this show, their costumes matched the one worn by Mitchell.[277]

Other musicals and comedies in which Mitchell appeared included *Song of Songs;* Otto Harbach, A. Seymour Brown, and Harry Lewis's

A Pair of Queens; as Kate Armitage in Charles Dickson's *Three Twins;* George M. Cohan's *Fifty Miles from Boston* and *The Little Millionaire;* Joseph E. Howard's *The Time, the Place, and the Girl;* as Nadina Pop-off in *The Chocolate Soldier;* as Yvonne Sherry in Hugo Felix and M. Ordonneau's adaptation of *Madame Sherry; Charlie's Aunt;* and Willie Collier's *The Man from Mexico* and *Are You a Mason?*[278]

Mitchell also portrayed Ethel Toscani in George Broadhurst's *The Price;* Miriam in Hubert Henry Davies's *The Outcast;* The Woman in Porter Emerson Browne's *A Fool There Was;* Ruth Jordon in *The Great Divide;* The Girl in Eugene Brieux's *Damaged Goods;* Gertrude Meyer in Jack Lait's *Help Wanted;* Nance Mayo in Owen Davis's *A Man's Game;* Ruth Belmar in *Branded;* Margaret Holt in Robert Baker and John Emerson's detective story *The Conspiracy;* doubled as Queen Sardalia and the Lady in Elinor Glynn's love drama *Three Weeks;* Cleve Kinkead's *Common Clay;* Bayard Veiller's *The Flight;* Robert McLaughlin's *The Eternal Magdalene;* Eugene Walter's *Just a Woman;* and Betty Amseley, the heroine, in Harold McGrath and Grace Livingston's *The Man on the Box.*[279] Reviewing her performance in *The Man on the Box,* White said, "The work of Abbie Mitchell as the heroine is of a character with her usual excellence."[280]

Mitchell was first seen on the screen in *The Scapegoat* (1917), co-starring Sidney Kirkpatrick. Produced by the Frederick Douglass Film Company of Jersey City, N.J., the film was written by Paul Laurence Dunbar. "There is more sustained dramatic interest in 'The Scapegoat' than any other Negro photo play that has yet been produced, and it easily takes rank as the best to date," reported the *New York Age.*[281] Mitchell was also seen in *Eyes of Youth* (1920) produced by the Quality Amusement Corporation.[282] In 1919 the Black owners of the Quality Amusement Corporation purchased the Lafayette Players and the Lafayette Theatre in Harlem, four companies of the Lafayette Players, and several Black theatres on the East Coast. By 1922, however, the Quality Amusement Corporation had lost most of its assets.[283]

In 1920, when "Jean de Reszke declared that she had a perfect mezzo-soprano voice, she became more and more famous as a recitalist in every major city of America and Europe."[284] In 1921 Mitchell toured with Cook's Southern Syncopated Orchestra (a.k.a. the New York Syncopated Orchestra) here and abroad. When Cook returned to the United States in 1921, Mitchell stayed in Europe touring with her act, "Abbie Mitchell and Her Full Harmonic Quartet." During her stay she again studied voice in Paris with Reszke and with Szbrilla, Reszke's teacher; she returned for more study in 1931.[285] "All my work as an actress has been done with my singing in mind," said Mitchell. "I learned that a singer must know dramatics, but I could not stop for a long course."[286]

10. Abbie Mitchell (c. 1920). Wife of Will Marion Cook, she played principal parts in the musicals: *Clorindy, The Origin of the Cakewalk* (1898), *In Dahomey* (1903), *The Southerners* (1904), *Bandana Land* (1908), and *The Red Moon* (1909). She made the transition to drama and became a member of the Lafayette Players. Other dramas in which she performed included *In Abraham's Bosom* (1926), *Stevedore* (1934), *The Little Foxes* (1939), and *On Whitman Avenue* (1946). A celebrated concert singer, she was the first Clara in *Porgy and Bess* (1935) where she introduced the song "Summertime." Photo courtesy of Schomburg Center for Research in Black Culture, The New York Public Library, Astor, Lenox and Tilden foundations.

By the early 1920s Mitchell and Cook had separated, and soon afterward divorced. They respected each other's talent, however, and remained friends. During this time, Mitchell began teaching voice. Hilda Simms and Maxine Sullivan attempted to study with Mitchell, but they were unable to get along with her. Adelaide Hall and Etta Moten did study with Mitchell, however.[287]

During the early 1920s, Mitchell studied acting with the well-known Jasper Deeter.[288] A producer, director, actor, and teacher, Deeter founded the Hedgerow Theatre in Moylan, Pennsylvania, in 1923.[289] Mitchell studied with Deeter during the same period as Ann Harding. Mitchell was never accepted by the other students at the Hedgerow. Some of them, including Harding, never spoke to her. Nonetheless, Mitchell returned to the Hedgerow many times to perform under Deeter's direction.[290] Moreover, Mitchell and Deeter would eventually work together in a landmark production on Broadway.

In 1924 Mitchell starred in *Negro Nuances,* produced by Will Marion Cook. This musical, with book by Abbie Mitchell and the performing/producing team of Flournoy E. Miller and Aubrey Lyles (who, along with Noble Sissle and Eubie Blake, had co-created *Shuffle Along* in 1921), featured music and lyrics by Cook. Although there is no information available to document place of performance or even musical numbers, "the play traces the musical history of blacks starting in Africa, moving with the slave ships, the lamentations of pre-civil war days to the reconstruction period as typified by the early minstrels of Jim Bland's day."[291]

In 1925 Mitchell was a principal in *Harlem Rounders.* This two-act musical was produced by Frank Montgomery, with J. Rosamond Johnson as the musical director. Act One included a scene in Dixie, a scene in Italy (in which Mitchell sang an Italian number, "Rose of Montmartre"), and a scene in Mexico. The second act included an Apache scene, a Charleston scene, an Old Broadway scene, a Monte Carlo scene, and a Russian scene. The Russian scene featured Mitchell, supported by the chorus, singing "Song of Songs."[292]

By 1926 Mitchell had married her second husband. He was a delicate, handsome young man many years her junior. By 1927 they had separated. Though it was not directly related to their breakup, he committed suicide. (No information was found regarding his name or the date of their marriage.)[293]

On 30 December 1926 Paul Green's *In Abraham's Bosom* opened at the Provincetown Theatre on Macdougal Street in New York. Set in the Turpentine district of North Carolina in 1885, Green's biographical tragedy depicts the struggles and defeat of Abraham McCraine. Abraham, the son of a Black mother and a White planter, Colonel McCraine,

realizes that education is the most effective way of truly emancipating
Blacks. Despite the apathy of his own people and the other planters,
his father helps him establish a school. When the Colonel dies, Abraham, his wife, son, and aunt are thrown off the land. After eighteen
years of wandering the Carolinas, Abraham returns to his hometown in
hopes that his half-brother will help him start another school. When
Lonnie McCraine not only refuses to help him but instead, robs him of
the land his father had willed him, Abraham kills his half-brother and
in turn is shot by the Ku Klux Klan. Abbie Mitchell played Muh Mack,
Abraham's aunt.[294]

Except for reporting that the play was too long and too realistic in
certain scenes, especially the whipping scene, the critics all agreed that
In Abraham's Bosom was an artistic success. "A sincere and powerful
tragedy written with courage, understanding, logic and humor, was
played last night by actors whose sincerity matched that of the author," wrote the reviewer for the *New York Times*.[295] He went on to say:

> ... the range runs all the way from the boisterous and infectious
> gayety of the race to the religious ecstasy and the madness of the
> mixed blood who is the central tragic figure. . . .
>
> Julius Bledsoe played the part of that black man— . . . He was
> especially impressive in the scene of religious exaltation when he
> prayed over the infant whom he dedicated to the saving of his
> people and in the mad scene after the murder his perfect solem-
> nity in the situations of comedy contributed enormously to the
> effects produced by the others—especially Abbie Mitchell as an
> old woman. . . .[296]

"Abbie Mitchell gives a flawless performance as the nagging but
well-intentioned aunt and crystallizes the promise she showed in *Deep
River,*" wrote Wilfred J. Riley.[297] According to George Goldsmith of the
Herald-Tribune, "you never saw anything more realistic in your life than
Abbie Mitchell's portrayal of the old aunt."[298] The reviewer for the *Telegram* said, "The Goldie McAllister of Rose McClendon, who will be remembered as a hit in 'Deep River'; the Muh Mack of Abbie Mitchell,
and the Douglas McCraine of R. J. Huey are other outstanding imper-
sonations of a performance which is capital from beginning to end."[299]
The *Evening Post* reported, "As the cackling and derisive aunt of Abraham, Abbie Mitchell is vivid and intelligent."[300]

J. A. Rogers, reviewing for the *Amsterdam News*, had this to say:

> At the Provincetown Theatre is again being demonstrated the
> fact that tragedy—real, searing tragedy—as poignant and grip-

ping as anything ever written by Shakespeare or Eschybis [Aeschylus?], is to be found in Negro life in America.

The play is a triumph not only for its author but its interpreters, . . . Abbie Mitchell acted the part of Muh Mack to perfection. . . .

Despite the fact that in its last analysis the play smacks of white man's interpretation, it reveals great understanding of what the aspiring Negro really faces in the South, and is in its effect a powerful plea for justice.[301]

According to the *Evening World*, "Miss Mitchell, as Abraham's aunt, was such a 'Mammy' as the stage seldom sees. She has no sympathy with her nephew in his unceasing struggle against poverty and oppression and lightens the most sordid parts of the drama with her comedy."[302] The New York *American* documented a pivotal transition for Mitchell: "The principal burden of the play is splendidly carried by Julius Bledsoe and Rose McClendon, featured in the late-lamented 'Deep River,' and Abbie Mitchell, who has been starring for the last five years in Harlem stock. This, by the way, is Miss Mitchell's first appearance in a straight colored role."[303]

The 13 February 1927 *New York Times* ran a sketch of Mitchell as Muh Mack. The caption read: "Abbie Mitchell in 'In Abraham's Bosom' Which Will Move from Macdougal Street to the Garrick Theatre Tomorrow Night."[304] On 5 March, 1927, after 72 performances, *In Abraham's Bosom* closed.[305]

On 21 April 1927, Leigh Hutty's *The House of Shadows* opened at the Longacre Theatre in New York for twenty-nine performances.[306] The play is about a Harvard psychologist, bent on exposing American ghosts, who rents an old mansion on the Hudson River because of a legend that no one ever entering the house came out alive. He, along with a young woman, discovers a pirate's treasure and escapes the house (which is filled with secret passageways and mysterious panels) after many horrifying adventures. Abbie Mitchell played Darkey's Wife and Tom Mosley, who was also seen in *In Abraham's Bosom*, played Darkey, the comic relief.[307]

Despite saying that the cast was generally good and that the audience enjoyed the stage devices, the reviews were generally unfavorable. "The only person who seemed real to us was Miss Abbie Mitchell as the Professor's faithful, intrepid colored servant," reported Stephen Rathbun. "She established a convincing characterization, but the other players were hardly more than shadows."[308]

Percy Hammond was negative: " 'The House of Shadows' is an exercise in nursery nightmares, being an enfant account of a haunted bungalow infested by pixies and hobgoblins. 'Rastus,' a Negro servant, trembled in a familiar fashion and the ingenue removed the stockings from her graceful limbs with no excuse whatsoever. Despite those advertisements my advice to *Herald-Tribune* playgoers is to beware of 'The House of Shadows.' It is not so good."[309]

On 8 May 1927, *In Abraham's Bosom* reopened at the Provincetown Theatre for a second engagement, with Anyce Francis replacing Mitchell as Muh Mack. During mid-May, after *The House of Shadows* closed, Mitchell took over the role of Muh Mack from Francis. On 19 June 1927, after fifty-one performances, *In Abraham's Bosom* closed again.[310]

In Abraham's Bosom became a huge personal success for its author, winning him the Pulitzer Prize in 1926. Despite its popularity, Loften Mitchell felt that the play was overrated: "For all of Mr. Green's sincerity and dramatic skill, *In Abraham's Bosom* is not a great play. It seems to have little relationship to the plight of the American Negro at that point in the nation's history. He presented to us a man named Abraham who attempted to 'elevate' his people through education. In the midst of all of this, Abraham has trouble with black people and white people and, of course, he ends up by killing a white man."[311]

The often mentioned *Deep River* in the *In Abraham's Bosom* reviews referred to Laurence Stallings and Frank Harling's native opera, featuring an integrated cast. Produced and staged by Arthur Hopkins, *Deep River* opened on 4 October 1926 at the Imperial Theatre in New York for 32 performances.[312] Set in New Orleans in 1835, the piece depicts a conflict among a Creole aristocrat, a quadroon girl, and her Kentucky lover during the annual ball.[313]

Rose McClendon is cited as having given an excellent performance as a proud but aging madam in a house of quadroon women.[314] Contrary to the 15 January 1927 review in *Billboard* by Wilfred J. Riley reporting that "Abbie Mitchell gives a flawless performance as the nagging but well-intentioned aunt and crystalizes the promise she showed in *Deep River*,"[315] neither the program nor any other review mentions Mitchell. It is possible that she did not appear in the show.

Like Laura Bowman, Mitchell had two Broadway openings in one season: *In Abraham's Bosom* and *The House of Shadows*. Also like Bowman, Mitchell, a fair-skinned woman, "blackened up" to play the parts. Further, in shows that featured White actors (except *On Whitman Avenue*), like Bowman, Mitchell played a servant. This was the role she would perform in all of the White productions in which she would appear.

On 8 November 1927 George Abbott and Ann Preston Bridgers's *Coquette* opened at Maxine Elliott's Theatre in New York and stayed on for 366 performances.[316] *Coquette* depicts the story of Norma Besant, a Carolina southern belle who falls in love with an outsider. When she becomes pregnant, her father avenges her honor by killing her lover. When her father is placed on trial for murder, in order to win him favor with the jury, Norma kills herself.[317] Helen Hayes was Norma Besant, and Charles Waldron was her father. Elliott Cabot played the outcast lover, and Abbie Mitchell portrayed Julia.

Staged by Abbott, *Coquette* was a hit. Helen Hayes, the star, received glowing reviews. Out of twenty available reviews, only two mentioned Abbie Mitchell. "Andrew Lawjor, Jr., Albert Smith and Abbie Mitchell were helpful," said Burns Mantle.[318] According to the *Evening Post:* ". . . it is not the atmosphere that is so impressive in inept native drama, but its bromidity and Mr. Abbott can let an old mammy, played admirably by Abbie Mitchell, lumber up stairs humming a spiritual to herself – can hold the whole stage, in fact, while she does it – and leave you thinking it a glorious accident, when you know perfectly well that the adroit Mr. Abbott has underscored it stunningly by refusing to underscore it at all."[319]

In 1927 Mitchell was forty-three years old. As documented by her portrayals in *In Abraham's Bosom* and *The House of Shadows,* she had already begun playing old mammy/servant roles. Influenced by her many experiences and years of professional training, Mitchell had developed into a very critical perfectionist. She neither associated with the other cast members socially nor considered them to be friends. Mitchell possessed a sharp tongue which she wielded like a weapon. It is reported that she intimidated her co-workers, both Black and White.[320]

Of all the actresses with whom Mitchell worked, she admired Helen Hayes most. One night during *Coquette*'s New York run, Ethel Barrymore came backstage to see Hayes. When Barrymore asked Hayes, "Who's that marvelous nigger back there (referring to Mitchell)?" Hayes, who both respected and feared Mitchell, responded frantically, "Please, Please, Oh God! Please don't let her hear you say that."[321]

After its New York run *Coquette,* starring Helen Hayes, went on the road. Abbie Mitchell toured with the company. They opened on 19 November 1928 at the Shubert Wilbur Theatre in Boston. On 27 January 1929 they began their sixth week at the Selwyn Theatre in Chicago. On 11 March 1929 they opened at the Shubert Alvin Theatre in Pittsburgh. By 19 March 1929 they were performing at the Cass Theatre in Detroit. On 22 April 1929 *Coquette* opened at Poli's Theatre in Washington, D.C. The last available program to list either Helen Hayes or Abbie Mitchell was the production that opened on 10 June 1929 at the Curran Theatre in San Francisco.[322]

As has been stated, the "New Lafayette Players" would arrive in Los Angeles from New York to open the 1929 Fall season at the Lincoln Theatre. On 23 September 1929, the group opened with George V. Hobart's *Experience*. Abbie Mitchell, one of the "new" stars from New York, starred in the show. According to Sister Thompson:

> Helen Ware, the Broadway actress who had played the role taken by Abbie Mitchell in the New York production of the play, attended the opening night performance. Miss Ware had nothing but praise for Abbie Mitchell and said in an interview that she considered Miss Mitchell a great actress. It was the first time that Miss Ware had witnessed the play from "out front" after having played her role for an entire year on Broadway, and she was happy to have been able to see Abbie Mitchell's performance.[323]

From 1931 to 1934 Abbie Mitchell was head of the vocal department at Tuskegee Institute,[324] the historic Black college in Alabama. Although she had no college degree, she possessed unquestionable talent, training, and professional experience. Nevertheless, she regretted not having completed her formal education, particularly because Cook's family was educated. His mother had been among the first Black women to graduate from Oberlin College in Ohio. According to her granddaughter (a retired New York City public school French teacher), Mitchell instilled in her the desire to get an education.[325]

While on the faculty at Tuskegee, Mitchell continued to perform on the concert stage in various cities. In Chicago, while on tour during the early part of 1931, Mitchell received a radio contract that had her singing nationwide. In that concert she sang a group of spirituals by Hall Johnson, William L. Dawson, and Will Marion Cook; translations of poems by Countee Cullen and Langston Hughes; American and English songs by La Forge, Nevin, and Bantock; French songs by Debussy, Hahn, Foundrain, Duparc, and Faure; and German songs by Pahlen.[326]

On 22 November 1931 she gave an all-Negro recital at Town Hall in St. Louis. The announcement read: "The Greatest Singer of the Present Day will appear in an all-Negro Song Recital."[327] "Abbie Mitchell," said the *St. Louis Argus*, "who has given convincing evidence in the past as a singer of German lieder, chose to devote her gifts Friday afternoon at the Town Hall to a program of songs by and of Negroes. Miss Mitchell was no less the artist in this type of music. She understands it as few others singers even of her race do."[328]

In a review of a concert in Pittsburgh, the *Pittsburgh Courier* raved: "Abbie Mitchell is the greatest singer of songs that the Negro has."[329]

Of her performance in Washington, the *Washington Tribune* reported:
"Prolonged applause greeted her rendition of Schubert's *Erlkoenig,*
Lied Der Mignon, (Schubert) was well received, as was Chausson's
Apaisement. But the enthusiasm of the audience knew no bounds when
she gave the impressively beautiful interpretation of the Aria Ritorna
Vincitor from *Aida* (Verdi)."[330]

About an earlier recital, Charles D. Isaacson of the *New York Morning Telegraph* (no date) wrote: "Her diction and handling of the German
group of songs was a feat: *Die Lorelei* of Liszt was memorable. Her
diction was a model of her white rivals. Followed the Ritorno Vincitor
from *Aida.* What an Aida this woman would make!"[331]

In 1933, after years of studying voice and opera, Mitchell remarked
about herself: "I have come from the dinge of smoke and heat, tired and
worn from singing, and lit the oil lamp. In quietude while my loved
ones slept, I dug down to the roots of French, German, Italian, theory,
harmony and counterpoint. – I have always studied and I still am
studying."[332]

In a 1934 interview printed in the *Pittsburgh Courier,* Mitchell as-
serted that there is a goal not yet attained: "a 'Negro opera,' produced
by a 'race man.' . . . But I'm so afraid it will eventually be a white person. The Metropolitan Opera House is a goal. The gates of that place
must be crashed yet by a Negro.' "[333] Mitchell's dream for the creation
of a "Negro opera" would soon come true, although it would not be written by a "race" man.

The Metropolitan Opera House hired Mitchell to sing the offstage
role of the child in Debussy's *Pelleas et Melisande.* She was not to be
seen on stage, however. During rehearsals, Mitchell "invited the 'dark-
est skinned' Black men she knew to her dressing room." When the management at the Met told her to stop, she left the company (no date
available).[334] Although she did not sing at the Met, Mitchell did perform in opera. In July 1934 she sang *Cavalleria Rusticana* at the Mecca
Temple in New York, and again in August with the Aeolian Opera Company.[335]

Abbie Mitchell returned to the legitimate theatre in 1934 in the role
of Bennie in Paul Peters and George Sklar's *Stevedore.* A drama of race
and labor problems, *Stevedore* opened at the Civic Repertory Theatre
in New York on 18 April 1934 where it ran for 110 performances.[336] Set
along the docks of a Southern seaport, the play centers around a Black
dock worker who is framed. He is falsely accused of raping a White
woman only because he is helping to organize a longshoremen's union.
With the help of some White friends, he escapes from the police. In
retaliation, other Whites riot against all the Blacks who live in the
alley.[337]

Produced by the militant Theatre Union, a labor group, *Stevedore,* according to the program notes, "is based on incidents which occurred during the attacks on Negroes in East St. Louis in 1919, the Chicago attacks in 1919, the Dr. Sweet case in Detroit, the Bogalusa lumber strike, the New Orleans dock strikes, the Colorado bathing beach fight, the attack on the Camp Hill, Ala., share croppers and the similar attack at Tuscaloosa, Ala."[338] "The white actors are good," wrote Brooks Atkinson, "but the Negroes give their scenes a robustiousness and an earthiness that are wholly exhilarating. . . . Many Negroes were in the audience last night, both downstairs and up. Their response to the lines and the incidents gave the play an entirely fresh meaning."[339]

After 100 performances, *Stevedore* closed for the summer. On 1 October 1934, *Stevedore* reopened at the Civic Repertory Theatre for a second engagement with Abbie Mitchell replacing Georgette Harvey as Bennie. The New York *World-Telegram* said, "Last night's audience, as was the first night audience on 'Stevedore's' original opening night, was vociferous in its sympathies with the negro laborers."[340]

"It is still a good show — violent, honest and stirring — and it accomplishes what it set out to do: it makes its audience reflective and more and a little uncomfortable," reported the New York *Evening Post.* "Jack Carter is superb in the leading role, . . . Leigh Whipper, Abbie Mitchell, Edna Thomas and Al Watts were also excellent in their characterizations."[341]

Stevedore opened on a Monday evening. It played throughout the week, plus Saturday and Sunday matinees. Prices for tickets at the Civic Repertory Theatre, located at 105 West 14th Street, were 30¢, 45¢, 60¢, 75¢, $1.00, and $1.50 respectively.[342] The actual production of *Stevedore* and the scale of prices for tickets reflected the aims of the Theatre Union:

Ninety per cent of the people are barred from the theatre, we believe, by high admission prices, and also, though perhaps they are unconscious of it, by the remoteness of the average run of plays from their lives and their fundamental problems.

The Theatre Union is building a theatre of the ninety per cent. A theatre which will try to reflect with honesty and vitality the economic, emotional and cultural conflicts in the experience of our audience. . . .

The Theatre Union will produce plays that have meaning for and bearing on the struggles and conflicts of our times. It does not expect that these plays will fall into the accepted social patterns. Its point of view is that there is but one constructive guide in the prevailing situation; the interests of the great masses of the people, the working people, the workers as a class.[343]

On 24 November 1934, after sixty-four performances, *Stevedore* closed again and went on the road.[344] On 10 December 1934 *Stevedore* opened at the Garrick Theatre in Philadelphia. The last available program is for the production that opened on Christmas eve at the Selwyn Theatre in Chicago.[345] According to one reviewer, "Jack Carter as the hero, Canada Lee as his courageous friend and Abbie Mitchell as a grim black fury . . . show you a convincingly human picture of levee laborers and their women."[346]

The 1930s, the period of the Great Depression, brought social protest and excitement to the American theatre. *Stevedore*, a realistic, protest drama, mirrored the conflicts of the time. As Loften Mitchell put it: "Negroes were shouting and screaming then, in theatre and out, demanding an end to injustices, demanding fair employment and fair housing. They recognized, in and out of the the theatre, the need for white support."[347]

As has been stated, Abbie Mitchell had been hoping for a "Negro" opera created by a Black man. She was aware of the lyrical and dramatic potential of Black life for the stage. On 10 October 1935 the "American folk opera" *Porgy and Bess* opened at the Alvin Theatre in New York where it played for 124 performances.[348] Produced by the Theatre Guild, *Porgy and Bess*, an adaptation of DuBose and Dorothy Heyward's drama *Porgy* (1927), was composed by George Gershwin, with libretto by DuBose Heyward, and lyrics by Ira Gershwin and Heyward.

Set in Catfish Row in Charleston, South Carolina, *Porgy and Bess* depicts the tragic romance of Porgy, a crippled Black beggar, and Bess, a beautiful woman who also loves the bully Crown. In the end Porgy murders Crown and Bess, who thinks Porgy has been arrested, leaves Catfish Row for the North. Porgy, a double amputee, pursues her in his goat-drawn packing-box chariot.[349] Abbie Mitchell, who introduced the song "Summer Time," played Clara, an inhabitant of Catfish Row.

" 'Porgy and Bess,' besides being a highly significant contribution to the American theatre, is also box office," proclaimed the critic for *Variety*. He added: "Abbie Mitchell is a fine Clara with her introductory lullaby, "Summer Time," one of the finer things. . . ."[350] The New York *American* raved, "The cast was excellent. . . . There was astonishing ensemble, and absolute correctness in pitch and rhythm revealed themselves anew as the musical birthright of the gifted colored race."[351]

Burns Mantle exclaimed, " 'Porgy and Bess,' which is pretty certain to prove one of the sensations of this theatre season, is so shot with climaxes, musical and dramatic, that it wore an applauding audience at the Alvin Theatre last night a bit ragged before the evening was over."[352]

Loften Mitchell saw the original production when he was a teenager. "I found its characters stereotypes and its music imitative and not nearly as moving as its source," he recalled. *Porgy and Bess* is a "work generally hailed by whites and disliked by many Negroes."[353]

The last performances of *Porgy and Bess* at the Alvin Theatre occurred during the week of 20 January 1936. The company began their second week at the Forrest Theatre in Philadelphia on 3 February 1936. The last available program of *Porgy and Bess* to list Mitchell as "Clara" was the 16 March 1936 production at the National Theatre in Washington, D.C.[354]

On 15 February 1939 Lillian Hellman's *The Little Foxes* opened at the National Theatre in New York for 410 performances.[355] The title of the play is taken from the Song of Songs in the Bible: " 'Take us the foxes, the little foxes, that spoil the vines; for the vines have tender grapes.' " Set in the South in 1900, *The Little Foxes*, a play of social and industrial tyranny, depicts how the Hubbard clan (Regina, Ben, Oscar, and Oscar's son Leo) schemes to bring a cotton factory to their town. The factory would be a very good investment because the Blacks and Whites would work cheaply, and they could be forced to work for even less money by pitting them against each other. Regina ends up owning most of the mill, but she loses her daughter, who decides to stay with Addie when her mother moves North.[356] Abbie Mitchell played Addie, the female servant.

Despite its incredible success, the play received mixed reviews. The critics agreed, however, that the acting was good. The *Herald-Tribune* said:

> Playing the central character of the drama, the ruthless Regina, Miss Tallulah Bankhead offers the finest performance of her local career, a portrayal that is honest, merciless and completely understanding. . . . Lesser roles are well managed by Miss Abbie Mitchell and John Marriott as the family servants. The settings, direction and costumes are excellent. "The Little Foxes" is an important and distinguished play, properly acted, and it is convincing proof of Miss Hellman's standing as a dramatist.[357]

"This is one of the best roles of Miss Bankhead's career and she is releasing all the stops in portraying it," wrote the *World Telegram*. "She is in superb company. . . . The two Negro players in the play, Abbie Mitchell and John Marriott, are 'way above just being good.' "[358]

According to Brooks Atkinson, "Tallulah . . . plays with superb command of the entire character—sparing of the showy side, constantly aware of the poisonous spirit within. . . . There are also vivid characterizations in the other parts by Charles Dingle, Abbie Mitchell, Carl Benton Reid, Dan Duryea, Lee Baker and John Marriott."[359]

"Regina as played by Miss Bankhead, is a splendid portrayal," wrote *Variety*. "Abbie Mitchell and John Marriott, as servants, are in the sterling cast."[360] The *Daily Worker* said: "Tallulah Bankhead has perhaps the best performance of her career as Regina Giddens, a greedy, unscrupulous and heartless woman. . . . Abbie Mitchell and John Marriott interpreted two Negro servants, as they were written, with sympathy, dignity and humor."[361]

According to Arthur Pollack of the *Brooklyn Daily Eagle:* "Addie . . . has the words for Miss Hellman's meaning. There are people in this world, she says, who eat the earth and the people upon it while others, who do not approve, stand about and do nothing to prevent them."[362]

When Mitchell auditioned for the role of Addie, Hellman told her that she had done very well, but she wanted a "dull Black" woman to play the part. Mitchell responded nastily, "I will never be 'dull Black.' " For three weeks she heard nothing from Hellman. After auditioning every Black actress who wanted the part, no one measured up to her. Mitchell was called back to show how she could look with burnt cork makeup. She played all of the performances in blackface. On the opening night of previews, Mitchell received numerous curtain calls. The next morning at rehearsals, Bankhead approached Mitchell. She told her, "I don't care who you are. This has got to be my show." As a result, many of Mitchell's lines were cut.[363]

Mitchell remained alone throughout the run of the show. She did not like anyone in the cast; she could barely tolerate Bankhead.[364] On 3 February 1940 *The Little Foxes* closed on Broadway and went on tour.[365] Mitchell left *The Little Foxes* in Chicago in 1940 to assist as technical advisor and to play the part of Abbie Mitchell, herself, in the American Negro Exposition's "Cavalcade of the Negro Theatre," written by Arna Bontemps and Langston Hughes.[366]

During this time Mitchell was living on Seventh Avenue between 116th and 117th Streets in New York with her boyfriend, her daughter, and her granddaughter. By this time her son was a professor at Howard University; she married her third husband (another man many years her junior) because her living arrangements lacked professional propriety. (No other information was found regarding her third husband.)[367]

During the 1940s Mitchell organized the Abbie Mitchell Players and began teaching drama in church basements and at the "Y" in Harlem. The company, which included her granddaughter, was still in existence in the 1950s.[368] According to Rosetta LeNoire, who studied acting with

Mitchell, "Abbie was the quiet 'Grand Dame of Drama,' and everybody went to her for acting lessons." During the 1930s and 1940s, Ethel Waters was the Black star most accepted by White audiences. Whenever she performed, big name White stars would attend. LeNoire revealed that when Black actors, including Ethel Waters, were cast in dramatic roles, "as soon as they received their scripts, they would run to Abbie Mitchell for coaching."[369]

On 8 May 1946, Maxine Wood's *On Whitman Avenue* opened at the Cort Theatre in New York for 150 performances.[370] Set in a pleasant White Northern suburb, *On Whitman Avenue* tells the story of a White storekeeper whose liberal daughter rents an apartment in the family home to a Black veteran and his family. The storekeeper, who bows to the pressures of his neighbors (who fear their property values will decrease) and the real estate company, evicts his Black tenants. Will Geer played the storekeeper, Canada Lee (who was also co-producer) was the veteran, and Abbie Mitchell, his mother.[371]

Because of its theme, the play aroused much controversy. Before the New York opening, *On Whitman Avenue* had played successfully in Detroit and Buffalo. According to a press release, the play had been "endorsed" by Eleanor Roosevelt and other prominent people.[372] Many of the critics, however, did not like the play.

Lewis Nichols of the *New York Times* said:

> Maxine Wood is writing about the Negro and the white, and how an antagonistic relationship can and does affect both. She is not a practiced playwright, and the final treatment of a difficult theme has eluded her. . . .
>
> Caught in the rather overpowering toils of the script, the players have difficulty in making their contributions seem real. . . . The play's aspirations are honest and sincere, but the effect grows increasingly disappointing.[373]

Ward Morehouse of the *Sun* wrote: "Quite the weakest of the racial problems plays that have come along this season."[374] Howard Barnes of the *Tribune* reported: "While it rates a high mark for sincerity, it is lean on theatrical effectiveness."[375] Robert Garland said: "If last night's play proves anything new – and I'm not so sure it does! – it proves that Canada Lee is more than ever to be reckoned with as a fine American actor."[376]

Other critics were favorably impressed. "Here it is, folks! That play on the Negro question for which we have all been waiting. What Miss Wood had done . . . is to bring her problem out in the open and to discuss it boldly and candidly and intelligently," proclaimed Vernon Rice

of the *Post.*[377] According to William Hawkins of the *Telegram:* "Comes
to tighter grips with the post war racial problem than any play so far
presented here. . . . Maxine Wood had the firm painstaking touch of a
Hellman."[378]

The 22 May 1945 issue of *Variety* devoted a column to the critical
reactions to *On Whitman Avenue.* It cited the editorial and column
printed in the 18 May 1946 *The People's Voice,* a Harlem weekly:

> In lead editorial headed "Lynching on Broadway," paper said "an-
> other excellent play of Negro life is in process of being lynched by
> the 'kept' dramatic critics on Broadway." Calling the play "a mag-
> nificent and stirring dramatic interpretation of the housing prob-
> lem faced by returning Negro GI vets," sheet said it could
> understand why "critics of the big business-dominated daily
> press" didn't like "Avenue." Their "anti-Negro prejudices" had al-
> ready been challenged by other Negro plays this season, it said,
> and the critics "simply could not stand up under 'Avenue's' indict-
> ment." Paper is inviting readers to a public forum May 31 to dis-
> cuss the play's merits.
>
> Fredi Washington, a Negro actress now running column as the
> sheet's theatrical editor, was still stronger in taking the critics to
> task by name. . . . She singled out John Chapman (News) for
> sloughing off the play, and Ward Morehouse (Sun) especially for
> his "phoney liberalism." "You, like most of your colleagues," she
> told Morehouse, "went around robin's red barn to try to cover up
> the fact that you, like Mrs. Tilden in the play, would probably be
> horrified at the thought that you might have to live in the same
> house or neighborhood with Negroes."
>
> Excepting Vernon Rice (Post), Arthur Pollack (Brooklyn Eagle),
> William Hawkins (World-Telegram) and Samuel Sillen (Daily
> Worker), Miss Washington ended: "You've made us mad boys."[379]

Regardless of the reviewers' criticism, Mitchell's notices were good.
According to Rice, "Canada Lee, . . . played David Bennett, the Negro
veteran with ease and touching naturalness. Abbie Mitchell and Augustus Smith, who played his mother and grandfather, Cora and
Gramp Bennett, respectively, have restraint, yet smothered intensity
that is exciting to watch."[380] In *Variety* Ibee stated: "Hilda Vaughn as
the friendly neighbor delivers whatever comedy there is. Others white
and colored who count are Vivienne Baber, Robert Simon, Philip
Clarke, Abbie Mitchell, Augustus Smith, Richard Williams, Kenneth
Terry and Martin Miller, latter three being kids."[381]

Robert Garland reported: "To make her point convincing, Maxine

Wood paints her blacks all white, her whites all black and stacks her cards exactly as she wants them. Apart from Will Geer, Abbie Mitchell and the flawless Mr. Lee, her players are equally contrived and unbelievable."[382] George Freedley, reviewing for the *Morning Telegraph,* wrote: "Abbie Mitchell as the mother of the colored family, Richard Williams as her [grand] son, and Augustus Smith . . . are outstanding."[383]

Mitchell was last seen on the stage in 1947 in *The Skull Boat,* starring Fay Bainter. (No other information available.) Poor eyesight prevented her from considering the role of Lena Younger (Mama) in Lorraine Hansberry's *A Raisin in the Sun.*[384]

The mother of a daughter, Marion, and a son, Mercer, Mitchell traveled a great deal during the years her children were growing up. Although she was conflicted regarding her role as a mother, Mitchell considered herself to have been a good parent. Most of the time, however, she lived in one place, while Mama Alice, the woman who had raised Mitchell, housed the children in another place. Even during those times when Mitchell lived in the same house with her children, Mama Alice was in charge of the household and of Marion and Mercer.[385]

Despite having earned a great deal of money during her career, Mitchell lived a "feast or famine" existence.[386] When she retired from the stage, she taught voice and acting in her studio on 125th Street in Harlem until around 1955 when her eyesight began to fail.[387] During this time Mitchell could not get an acting job; she was too old. In order to make ends meet, she worked in Francis Reckling's Record Shop on 125th Street selling sheet music.[388]

On 16 March 1960, after a long illness, Abbie Mitchell died in Harlem Hospital in New York City.[389] According to "Abbie Mitchell Goes to Perpetual 'Summertime,' " the obituary in the *Amsterdam News:* "They sang the songs Abbie Mitchell made famous during her career in the theatre and on the concert stage at a memorial service held Sunday afternoon." Former Executive Secretary of the Negro Actors Guild of America, Mitchell is buried in St. Raymond's Cemetery in the Bronx, and she is survived by three grandchildren.[390]

Abbie Mitchell, the quintessential Black actress, had a career that lasted nearly fifty years. Like so many of her contemporaries, she first sang on the professional stage in musicals before going on to act in dramatic roles. Through her association with the Lafayette Players and her own amateur acting groups, Mitchell helped to foster the development of Black Theatre. Further, throughout her career, she performed in landmark productions that made theatrical history for Blacks and for the American stage. As demonstrated by her success as both a serious singer and actress, Mitchell possessed unquestionable talent and determination. "Her life epitomized the paradox that beset Negro artists who knew the glamour of the early 1900s and were idolized by European audiences, sovereigns and Harlem theatre-goers, but denied total American acceptance."[391]

5
EPILOGUE: THE LEGACY

By the turn of the century, some Blacks were beginning to integrate into mainstream American society. In a historical context, the emergence of the Black dramatic actress coincides with the attitudes of a changing society and parallels the breakthroughs in other areas. The emergence of Black women performers during this period gave birth to a new generation of theatre artists, adding a new dimension to the American theatre scene. The inclusion of women in Black theatricals marked a turning point in Black participation in American theatre. With sophistication and style, they helped to change the stereotypical image, opening up for women numerous possibilities on the professional stage. Through beauty, talent, spirit, and determination, they led the way to the acceptance of Black performers, particularly women, around the world.

These Black women pioneers helped to lay the foundation for contemporary Black actresses. This is not to say that all Black women acting in drama by 1917 began their careers in musicals, but when given the opportunity to perform in other than stereotypical roles, those theatre professionals who began in musicals possessed many years of experience and training. They stepped easily from musicals to dramas, establishing themselves as role models for contemporary Black dramatic actresses. Through their association with the Lafayette Players, they helped to foster the development of Black theatre. In addition to organizing their own acting troupes Laura Bowman, Abbie Mitchell, and Anita Bush trained and coached some of the top Black actors of the 1930s and 1940s. By helping to provide trained talent, they made a significant contribution to mainstream American theatre.

Stemming from minstrelsy, the next form of theatre accessible to Blacks was the musical stage. Despite its contributions, *The Creole Show* performed a disservice to Black women performers: It helped to foster and preserved the "lightskinned woman" image over the years, which tends to exclude "darkskinned" Black women from certain roles. For the most part, the Black chorus girls of the 1920s and 1930s were fairskinned. The legendary Cotton Club in Harlem was noted for its "high yellow" chorus line.

Traditionally, musicals have been able to attract Broadway producers and audiences. Due to the nature of musicals, which incorporate large choruses, a number of female singers and dancers have been able to obtain work. Until recently, however, they were usually "lightskinned."

When turn-of-the-century Black actresses made the transition from musicals to dramas, the majority of their roles (which were written by White authors) were as servants. At the time these women entered the theatre, a light complexion was preferred. Ironically, thirty years later, when the stage image changed from "glorified 'coloured' girl" to "mammy," so did the complexion. In order to play certain roles, these women had to "blacken up," their skin color working for or against them at different times. Though minstrelsy had disappeared, these actresses had to "make up" to conform to the expectations of their White patrons. Given that this situation continued, Abbie Mitchell (who played Addie in *The Little Foxes*) was able to project some kind of independent spirit that lay outside the traditional character. In order to work, early Black actresses had to appeal to a predominantly White audience. Despite having had to compromise, they managed to bring humanity to the characters. They were artists. In the spirit of keeping on, they not only survived, but flourished.

Like these women, Ethel Waters made a name for herself as a singer/ dancer before appearing in dramatic roles. One of her most successful Broadway portrayals was that of Bernice Sadie Brown, the family servant, in Carson McCullers's *The Member of the Wedding* (1950). Though the show was a hit, Waters's part, according to Loften Mitchell, was little more than a "glorified mammy."[1] As recently as 1989 the play was revived, with Esther Rolle playing the part created by Waters.

The legacy of the early Black actress, like her life, was severely impacted by racism. Historically, some of the problems of race relations in America have been demonstrated by the roles Black women are forced to play on the professional stage. Faced with double discrimination, that of race and sex, Black actresses have been generally restricted to performing within a prescribed framework that permitted only limited opportunity.

At the turn of the century, Black entertainers achieved significant progress in redefining their stage images. By shattering some stereotypes, however, others are created. Given that the situation, in many ways, remains the same, Black performers today are still struggling to broaden their acceptance in "non-traditional" roles. Trained Black actresses are available to portray the same characters (though they are limited) as their White counterparts, if given the chance.

The American theatre has lagged in its responsibility to reflect the pluralism of the nation and its experiences. The issues of cross-cultural writing and non-traditional casting need to be addressed as ways of promoting performing opportunities for Black actresses. One hopes that as more Black men and women become involved in producing and writing, more plays will be provided that depict Black female characters, whether they be "wonderful or terrifying," who are truthful reflections of the lives of Black women.

NOTES

PREFACE

1. Richard Moody, *Dramas from the American Theatre, 1762–1909* (Cleveland, OH: The World Publishing Co., 1966), 309–13.
2. Yvonne Shafter, "Black Actors in the Nineteenth Century American Theatre," *CLA Journal* 20, no. 3 (March 1977): 400.

INTRODUCTION

1. Gerda Lerner, *The Black Woman in American History* (Menlo Park, CA: Addison-Wesley, 1971), 70.
2. August Meier, *Negro Thought in America 1880–1915* (Ann Arbor, MI: University of Michigan Press, 1969), 20.
3. Ibid.
4. Ibid.
5. Ibid., 20–21.
6. Ibid., 21–24.
7. W.E.B. Du Bois, *The Souls of Black Folk* (Chicago: A. C. McClury, 1903; reprinted, New York: The New American Library, 1969), 45.
8. LaFrances Rodgers-Rose, *The Black Woman* (Beverly Hills, CA: Sage Publications, 1980), 22.
9. Paula Giddings, *When and Where I Enter: The Impact of Black Women on Race and Sex in America* (New York: William Morrow, 1984), 137.
10. Rodgers-Rose, *The Black Woman*, 23.
11. Andrew Billingsley, *Black Families in White America* (Englewood Cliffs, NJ: Prentice-Hall, 1968), 16.
12. Gerda Lerner, *The Majority Finds Its Past* (New York: Oxford University Press, 1979), 74.
13. Ibid., 74–75.

14. Rodgers-Rose, *The Black Woman,* 23.

15. Giddings, *When and Where I Enter,* 79–80.

16. Seth M. Scheiner, *Negro Mecca: A History of the Negro in New York City* (New York: New York University Press, 1965), 48, 54–55, 57–58.

17. Gerda Lerner, ed., *Black Women in White America* (New York: Pantheon Books, 1972), 220.

18. Giddings, *When and Where I Enter,* 76.

19. Lerner, *Majority Finds Its Past,* 67–68.

20. Giddings, *When and Where I Enter,* 76.

21. Ibid., 77–78.

22. Lerner, *Majority Finds Its Past,* 72.

23. Giddings, *When and Where I Enter,* 82–83, 86.

24. Ibid.

25. Ibid., 85.

26. Ibid.

27. Ibid.

28. Ibid., 88.

29. Ibid., 22–23.

30. Ibid., 23.

31. Ibid., 24.

32. Ibid., 29.

33. Ibid., 28–29.

34. Ibid., 30.

35. Ibid., 90.

36. Ibid., 90–91.

37. Ibid., 92.

38. Ibid.

39. Ibid., 92–96.

40. Lerner, *Black Women in White America,* 440.

41. Giddings, *When and Where I Enter,* 95–135.

42. Ibid., 100.

43. Ibid., 135–37.

44. Ibid., 136.

45. Ibid., 137.

46. Jeanne-Marie Miller, "Images of Black Women in Plays by Black Playwrights," *CLA Journal* 20, no. 4 (June 1977): 494.

47. Ibid.

48. Arthur Quinn, *A History of the American Drama from the Beginning to the Civil War* (New York: Harper & Bros., 1923), 132.

49. Ibid.

50. Ibid., 333.

51. Shafter, "Black Actors in the Nineteenth Century," 388–89.

52. Helen Armstead-Johnson, *Black America on Stage* (New York: CASTA, The Graduate School and University Center of CUNY, 1978), 5.

53. Quoted in Herbert Marshall and Mildred Stock, *Ira Aldridge: The Negro Tragedian* (Carbondale, IL: Southern Illinois University Press, 1968), 33–34.

54. George C. D. Odell, *Annals of the New York Stage* (New York: Columbia University Press, 1928), 3:35.

55. Langston Hughes and Milton Meltzer, *Black Magic: A Pictorial History of the Negro in American Entertainment* (Englewood Cliffs, NJ: Prentice-Hall, 1968), 42.

56. Quoted in ibid.

57. Quoted in Marshall and Stock, *Ira Aldridge,* 35.

58. Quoted in ibid., 36.

59. Ibid.

60. Shafter, "Black Actors in the Nineteenth Century," 392.

61. Marshall and Stock, *Ira Aldridge,* 36.

62. Odell, *Annals of the New York Stage,* 3:71.

63. Ibid., 3:594.

64. Shafter, "Black Actors in the Nineteenth Century," 395.

65. Quoted in Marshall and Stock, *Ira Aldridge,* 39.

66. Ibid., 36–37.

67. Tom Fletcher, *100 Years of the Negro in Show Business* (New York: Burdge, 1954), xvii.

68. James Weldon Johnson, *Black Manhattan* (New York: Alfred A. Knopf, 1940; reprinted, New York: Arno Press and the *New York Times,* 1968), 89.

69. Margaret Butcher, *The Negro in American Culture,* 2d ed. (New York: Alfred A. Knopf, 1972), 25.

70. Robert Toll, *On with the Show: The First Century of Show Business in America* (New York: Oxford University Press, 1976), 23.

71. Allan Morrison, "One Hundred Years of Negro Entertainment," in *Anthology of the American Negro in the Theatre,* vol. 5 of *International Library of Negro Life and History,* edited by Lindsay Patterson (New York: Publishers Co., 1967–68), 4.

72. Loften Mitchell, *Black Drama: The Story of the American Negro in the Theatre* (New York: Hawthorn Books, 1967), 32.

73. Lynne Emery, *Black Dance in the United States from 1619 to 1970* (New York: Dance Horizons, 1980), 205.

74. Mitchell, *Black Drama,* 33.

75. Toll, *On with the Show,* 154.

76. Ibid., 155.

77. Morrison, "One Hundred Years of Negro Entertainment," 4.

78. Fletcher, *100 Years of the Negro in Show Business,* 103.

79. Toll, *On with the Show,* 155.

80. Emery, *Black Dance in the United States,* 206.

81. Fletcher, *100 Years of the Negro in Show Business,* xx.

82. Edith Isaacs, *The Negro in the American Theatre* (New York: Theatre Arts, 1947; reprinted, College Park, MD: McGarth, 1968), 28.

83. Ibid., 31.

84. Nathan Huggins, *Harlem Renaissance* (New York: Oxford University Press, 1971), 274–75.

85. Langston Hughes, "Black Influences in the American Theater, Part I,"

in *The Black American Reference Book,* edited by Mabel M. Smythe (Englewood Cliffs, NJ: Prentice-Hall, 1976), 688.

86. Willa Estelle Daughtry, *Sissieretta Jones: A Study of the Negro's Contribution to Nineteenth Century American Concert and Theatrical Life* (Ann Arbor, MI: University Microfilms, 1968), 90.

87. Jack Poggi, *Theater in America: The Impact of Economic Forces, 1879–1967* (Ithaca, NY: Cornell University Press, 1968), 5–15.

88. Ibid.

89. Ibid., 18–19.

90. Emery, *Black Dance in the United States,* 219–220.

91. Henry T. Sampson, *Blacks in Blackface: A Source Book on Early Black Musical Shows* (Metuchen, NJ: Scarecrow Press, 1980), 14.

92. Toll, *On with the Show,* 138.

93. Morrison, "One Hundred Years of Negro Entertainment," 5.

94. Robert Toll, *Blacking Up: The Minstrel Show in Nineteenth-Century America* (New York: Oxford University Press, 1974), 219.

95. Fletcher, *100 Years of the Negro in Show Business,* 42.

96. Toll, *On with the Show,* 128.

97. Ibid., 129.

98. Morrison, "One Hundred Years of Negro Entertainment," 5.

99. Toll, *On with the Show,* 129–130.

100. Morrison, "One Hundred Years of Negro Entertainment," 5, 7.

101. Helen Armstead-Johnson, "Blacks in Vaudeville: Broadway and Beyond," in *American Popular Entertainment,* edited by Myron Matlaw (Westport, CT: Greenwood Press, 1979), 77.

102. Morrison, "One Hundred Years of Negro Entertainment," 5.

103. Sister M. Francesca Thompson, "The Lafayette Players, 1917–1932," in *The Theater of Black Americans,* vol. 2., edited by Errol Hill (Englewood Cliffs, NJ: Prentice-Hall, 1980), 19–20, 22.

104. Huggins, *Harlem Renaissance,* 293.

105. Sister Thompson, "The Lafayette Players, 1917–1932," 27.

106. Johnson, *Black Manhattan,* 175.

107. Carl Van Vechten, "The Negro Theatre," in *"Keep A-Inchin' Along": Selected Writings of Carl Van Vechten about Black Art and Letters,* edited by Bruce Kellner (Westport, CT: Greenwood Press, 1979), 25–26.

108. Ibid., 27.

109. Freda L. Scott, "Black Drama and the Harlem Renaissance," *Theatre Journal* 37 (December 1985), 433.

110. Quoted in ibid.

1. THE BLACK FEMALE ARTIST AND THE AMERICAN STAGE PRIOR TO 1890

1. Toll, *On with the Show,* 41.

2. Rayford W. Logan and Michael Winston, eds., *Dictionary of American Negro Biography* (New York: W. W. Norton, 1982), 268.

3. Ibid.

4. Elizabeth T. Greenfield, *A Brief Memoir of the "Black Swan"* (London: n.p., 1853), 5.

5. Ibid., 6, 7.

6. Quoted in ibid., 7.

7. Quoted in ibid., 8.

8. Quoted in ibid., 10.

9. Quoted in ibid., 11.

10. Ibid., 8–9.

11. Quoted in ibid., 11.

12. Toll, *On with the Show*, 155.

13. Quoted in Greenfield, *Memoir of the "Black Swan,"* 14.

14. Philip S. Foner, *The Life and Writings of Frederick Douglass* (New York: International Publishers, 1950), 1:437.

15. Quoted in Greenfield, *Memoir of the "Black Swan,"* 14.

16. Quoted in ibid., 14–15.

17. Logan and Winston, eds., *Dictionary of American Negro Biography*, 269.

18. Greenfield, *Memoir of the "Black Swan,"* 16.

19. Quoted in Logan and Winston, eds., *Dictionary of American Negro Biography*, 270.

20. Ibid.

21. Errol Hill, "The Hyers Sisters." Paper delivered at the 4th Annual National Conference on Afro-American Theatre, Morgan State College, Baltimore, MD, April 1987, 2.

22. Ibid., 2–3.

23. Maude Cuney-Hare, *Negro Musicians and Their Music* (Washington, D.C.: Associated Publishers, 1936), 215–16.

24. Ibid., 216.

25. Eileen Southern, *Biographical Dictionary of Afro-American and African Musicians* (Westport, CT: Greenwood Press, 1982), 192.

26. Quoted in Cuney-Hare, *Negro Musicians and Their Music*, 216.

27. Quoted in ibid., 216–17.

28. Quoted in ibid., 217.

29. Southern, *Biographical Dictionary of Afro-American and African Musicians*, 192.

30. Cuney-Hare, *Negro Musicians and Their Music*, 217.

31. Southern, *Biographical Dictionary of Afro-American and African Musicians*, 192.

32. Sampson, *Blacks in Blackface*, 393.

33. Henry T. Sampson, *The Ghost Walks: A Chronological History of Blacks in Show Business, 1865–1910* (Metuchen, NJ: Scarecrow Press, 1988), 72, 73.

34. Hill, "The Hyers Sisters," 8.

35. The handwritten manuscript is located in the Rare Book Collection, Library of Congress, Washington, D.C. James V. Hatch and Omanii Abdullah, *Black Playwrights 1823–1977* (New York: R. R. Bowker, 1977), 123.

36. Southern, *Biographical Dictionary of Afro-American and African Musicians*, 192.

37. Hill, "The Hyers Sisters," 9.

38. Ibid., 9–10.

39. Ibid., 14.

40. Southern, *Biographical Dictionary of Afro-American and African Musicians,* 192.

41. Ibid.

42. Ibid.

43. Sampson, *The Ghost Walks,* 73.

44. Sampson, *Blacks in Blackface,* 23.

45. Southern, *Biographical Dictionary of Afro-American and African Musicians,* 192.

46. Sampson, *Blacks in Blackface,* 399.

47. Quoted in ibid.

48. Southern, *Biographical Dictionary of Afro-American and African Musicians,* 192.

49. Cuney-Hare, *Negro Musicians and Their Music,* 218.

50. Hill, "The Hyers Sisters," 12.

51. Ibid., 14.

52. Cuney-Hare, *Negro Musicians and Their Music,* 220–21.

53. Southern, *Biographical Dictionary of Afro-American and African Musicians,* 334.

54. Cuney-Hare, *Negro Musicians and Their Music,* 222.

55. Ibid., 223.

56. Quoted in ibid.

57. Quoted in ibid.

58. Southern, *Biographical Dictionary of Afro-American and African Musicians,* 334.

59. Ibid.

60. Ibid.

61. Ibid., 334–35.

62. Ibid.

63. Cuney-Hare, *Negro Musicians and Their Music,* 225.

64. Ibid., 214–15, 225.

65. Sampson, *Blacks in Blackface,* 68.

66. Cuney-Hare, *Negro Musicians and Their Music,* 215.

67. Ibid.

68. Ibid., 219–20.

69. Errol Hill, *Shakespeare in Sable: A History of Black Shakespearean Actors* (Amherst, MA: University of Massachusetts Press, 1984), 44.

70. Ibid., 45.

71. Ibid.

72. Lawson A. Scruggs, *Women of Distinction* (Raleigh, NC: L. A. Scruggs, 1893), 86–87.

73. Hill, *Shakespeare in Sable,* 65.

74. Scruggs, *Women of Distinction,* 87.

75. Quoted in Hill, *Shakespeare in Sable,* 65.

76. Ibid., 66–67.

77. Quoted in ibid., 68.

78. Quoted in ibid., 69.
79. Ibid., 72.
80. Scruggs, *Women of Distinction,* 87.
81. Hill, *Shakespeare in Sable,* 72.
82. Ibid., 72–73, 75.
83. Ibid., 75.
84. Ibid., 76.

2. GLORIFIED "COLOURED" GIRLS

1. According to Henry T. Sampson, this production originated from an idea conceived by Sam Lucas, the dean of Black theatrical artists at the turn of the century. In 1873 Sam became a member of the original Georgia Minstrels as a ballad singer. After leaving the Hyers Sisters, he performed as a comedian/singer/dancer in vaudeville. Until 1879, he played the part of Uncle Tom in *Uncle Tom's Cabin.* Lucas, the first Black man to do so, also played the same role in the film version of *Uncle Tom's Cabin* (1915). During the 1880s, while still performing his solo act, he met and married his second wife, Carrie Melvin. She, a concert musician and contralto soloist, and Lucas formed the musical act "Mr. and Mrs. Sam Lucas," and played all the major variety halls. It was during this time that Sam envisioned producing a Creole show. Unable to interest Black investors, Lucas approached Sam T. Jack, a White man who agreed to organize and finance the show, headed by Lucas and his wife (*Blacks in Blackface,* 6, 393–94).
2. James Weldon Johnson, *Black Manhattan* (New York: Alfred A. Knopf, 1940; reprinted, New York: Arno Press and *New York Times,* 1968), 89.
3. Ibid., 95.
4. Quoted in Sampson, *Blacks in Blackface,* 7.
5. Johnson, *Black Manhattan,* 95–96.
6. Fletcher, *100 Years of the Negro in Show Business,* 103.
7. Ibid.
8. Lynne Emery, "Black Dance and the American Musical Theatre to 1930," in *Musical Theatre in America,* edited by Glenn Loney (Westport, CT: Greenwood Press, 1984), 306.
9. Quoted in Marshall Stearns and Jean Stearns, *Jazz Dance: The Story of American Vernacular Dance.* 2d ed. (New York: Macmillan, 1970), 124.
10. Johnson, *Black Manhattan,* 96.
11. Sampson, *Blacks in Blackface,* 24, 62.
12. Johnson, *Black Manhattan,* 96–97. There is some confusion about the name of this theatre during that period. It was called both Palmer's and Wallack's.
13. Sampson, *Blacks in Blackface,* 448.
14. Quoted in ibid., 63–65.
15. Ibid., 68.
16. Johnson, *Black Manhattan,* 97–98.
17. Sampson, *Blacks in Blackface,* 68.
18. Helen Armstead-Johnson, "Themes and Values in Afro-American Li-

brettos and Book Musicals, 1898–1930," in *Musical Theatre in America,* edited by Glenn Loney, 134.

19. Johnson, *Black Manhattan,* 101.

20. Allen Woll, *Black Musical Theatre: From "Coontown" to "Dreamgirls"* (Baton Rouge, LA: Louisiana State University Press, 1989), 12, 13.

21. Armstead-Johnson, "Themes and Values in Afro-American Librettos," 134.

22. *New York Dramatic Mirror,* 9 April 1898, 16.

23. Woll, *Black Musical Theatre,* 171.

24. Sampson, *Blacks in Blackface,* 321.

25. Hughes and Meltzer, *Black Magic,* 46–47.

26. Huggins, *Harlem Renaissance,* 276.

27. Emery, *Black Dance in the United States,* 210.

28. Gerald Brodman, *The American Musical Theatre: A Chronicle* (New York: Oxford University Press, 1978), 159.

29. Emery, *Black Dance in the United States,* 210.

30. Southern, *Biographical Dictionary of Afro-American and African Musicians,* 275.

31. Ann Charters, *Nobody: The Story of Bert Williams* (New York: Macmillan, 1970), 35.

32. Sandra L. Richards, "Bert Williams: The Man and the Masks," *Mime, Mask & Marionette* 1 (Spring 1978): 13.

33. Sampson, *The Ghost Walks,* 224.

34. Sampson, *Blacks in Blackface,* 402, 438. I am using Ada because that is the name by which she was most commonly known, although she herself used Aida at one time.

35. Allen Woll, *The Dictionary of the Black Theatre: Broadway, Off-Broadway, and Selected Harlem Theatre* (Westport, CT: Greenwood Press, 1983), 155.

36. Sampson, *Blacks in Blackface,* 402.

37. Ibid., 438.

38. Van Vechten, "The Negro Theatre," 23.

39. Johnson, *Black Manhattan,* 107.

40. Helen Armstead-Johnson, "*Shuffle Along:* Keynote of the Harlem Renaissance," in *Theater of Black Americans,* vol. 1, edited by Errol Hill (Englewood Cliffs, NJ: Prentice-Hall, 1980), 128.

41. Woll, *Dictionary of the Black Theatre,* 86.

42. Johnson, *Black Manhattan,* 104–6.

43. Armstead-Johnson, "*Shuffle Along:* Keynote of the Harlem Renaissance," 129.

44. Richards, "Bert Williams," 14.

45. Helen Armstead-Johnson, *Black America on Stage* (New York: CASTA, The Graduate School and University Center of CUNY, 1978), 14.

46. Sampson, *Blacks in Blackface,* 347.

47. Ibid.

48. Edward Mapp, *Directory of Blacks in the Performing Arts* (Metuchen, NJ: Scarecrow Press, 1978), 36.

49. Sampson, *Blacks in Blackface,* 364.

50. Quoted in Woll, *Dictionary of the Black Theatre,* 156.

51. Ibid., 3.

52. Harry A. Poloski and Ernest Kaiser, comps., *The Negro Almanac,* 2d ed. (New York: Bellwether, 1971), 1095.

53. Woll, *Dictionary of the Black Theatre,* 146–47.

54. Sampson, *Blacks in Blackface,* 354.

55. Charters, *Nobody,* 96.

56. Quoted in ibid.

57. Sampson, *Blacks in Blackface,* 147.

58. Logan and Winston, eds., *Dictionary of American Negro Biography,* 442.

59. Sampson, *Blacks in Blackface,* 287.

60. Woll, *Dictionary of the Black Theatre,* 135.

61. Quoted in Charters, *Nobody,* 108.

62. Ibid., 107–108.

63. Sampson, *Blacks in Blackface,* 263.

64. Woll, *Dictionary of the Black Theatre,* 78.

65. Quoted in ibid.

66. Sampson, *Blacks in Blackface,* 439.

67. Woll, *Black Musical Theatre,* 56.

68. Isaacs, *The Negro in the American Theatre,* 44.

69. Sister Francesca Thompson, *The Lafayette Players, 1915–1932: America's First Dramatic Stock Company* (Ann Arbor, MI: University Microfilms, 1972), 251–52.

70. Sampson, *Blacks in Blackface,* 122.

71. Johnson, *Black Manhattan,* 170–71.

72. Ibid., 89.

73. James Haskins, *Black Theater in America* (New York: Thomas Y. Crowell, 1982), 55.

74. Quoted in ibid., 56.

75. F. H., "After the Play," *The New Republic* (14 April 1917): 325.

76. "Three Negro Plays," *New York Dramatic Mirror,* 14 April 1917, 7.

77. Lester A. Walton, "Negro Actors Make Debut in Drama at Garden Theatre; Given Most Cordial Welcome," *New York Age,* 12 April 1917, 1, 6.

78. Quoted in Daughtry, *Sissieretta Jones,* 126, 27.

79. Quoted in ibid., 128.

80. Isaacs, *The Negro in the American Theatre,* 57.

81. Burns Mantle and Garrison P. Sherwood, *The Best Plays of 1909–1919* (New York: Dodd, Mead, and Co., 1933), 598.

82. Richards, "Bert Williams," 15.

83. Ibid.

84. Armstead-Johnson, "Themes and Values in Afro-American Librettos," 133.

85. John Graziano, "Sentimental Songs, Rags, and Transformations: The Emergence of the Black Musical, 1895–1910," in *Musical Theatre in America,* edited by Glenn Loney, 211, 213, 231.

86. Ibid., 231.

87. James V. Hatch, "A Guide to 200 Years of Drama," *The Drama Review* 16 (December 1972): 18.

3. THE CLASS ACTS

1. Stearns and Stearns, *Jazz Dance*, 285.
2. Ibid.
3. Sampson, *Blacks in Blackface*, 381–82.
4. Fletcher, *100 Years of the Negro in Show Business*, 110, 112.
5. Sampson, *Blacks in Blackface*, 382.
6. Stearns and Stearns, *Jazz Dance*, 286.
7. Sampson, *Blacks in Blackface*, 382.
8. *Variety,* 5 February 1915 (Dora Dean Clippings: The Billy Rose Theatre Collection, The New York Public Library at Lincoln Center, Astor, Lenox and Tilden Foundations, hereafter referred to as Lincoln Center).
9. *Vanity Fair,* Dora Dean Clippings, Lincoln Center.
10. Fletcher, *100 Years of the Negro in Show Business*, 112.
11. Stearns and Stearns, *Jazz Dance*, 286.
12. Sampson, *Blacks in Blackface*, 382.
13. Stearns and Stearns, *Jazz Dance*, 286.
14. Ibid.
15. "Dora Dean and Co.," *Variety,* 26 June 1914, Dora Dean Clippings, Lincoln Center.
16. *Minneapolis Journal,* 23 July 1914, Dora Dean Clippings, Lincoln Center.
17. Fletcher, *100 Years of the Negro in Show Business*, 112.
18. Sampson, *Blacks in Blackface*, 383.
19. Fletcher, *100 Years of the Negro in Show Business*, 112.
20. Sampson, *Blacks in Blackface*, 383.
21. Stearns and Stearns, *Jazz Dance*, 285.
22. Ibid., 75.
23. Carl R. Gross, M.D., "A Brief History of the Life of Matilda Sissieretta (Joynor) Jones, 'The Black Patti' (1869–1933)," Moorland-Spingarn Research Center, Manuscript Department, Howard University, Washington, D.C., 1.
24. Ann Charters, *Nobody: The Story of Bert Williams* (New York: Macmillan, 1970), 44.
25. Gross, "The Black Patti," 3.
26. Ibid.
27. Ibid., 2.
28. Charters, *Nobody,* 44.
29. Gross, "The Black Patti," 3.
30. Logan and Winston, eds., *Dictionary of American Negro Biography,* 367.
31. Gross, "The Black Patti," 2.
32. Johnson, *Black Manhattan,* 100.
33. Daughtry, *Sissieretta Jones,* 145, 161.
34. Johnson, *Black Manhattan,* 100.
35. Gross, "The Black Patti," 2.
36. Daughtry, *Sissieretta Jones,* 142.
37. Gross, "The Black Patti," 1.

38. Ibid., 2.
39. Quoted in Daughtry, *Sissieretta Jones,* 146.
40. Ibid., 25.
41. Quoted in ibid., 149.
42. Quoted in ibid., 159.
43. "Echoes and Artifacts," Exhibit, Lincoln Center, 1 December 1990.
44. Quoted in Gross, "The Black Patti," 2.
45. Sampson, *Blacks in Blackface,* 386.
46. Daughtry, *Sissieretta Jones,* 90.
47. Johnson, *Black Manhattan,* 100–101.
48. Sampson, *Blacks in Blackface,* 9.
49. Johnson, *Black Manhattan,* 101.
50. Hill, "The Hyers Sisters," 14.
51. Quoted in Sampson, *Blacks in Blackface,* 387.
52. Ibid., 68.
53. Charters, *Nobody,* 45.
54. Gross, "The Black Patti," 2.
55. Stearns and Stearns, *Jazz Dance,* 85.
56. Daughtry, *Sissieretta Jones,* 96.
57. Quoted in ibid., 99.
58. Ibid., 100.
59. Quoted in ibid.
60. Quoted in ibid., 112.
61. Ibid., 106.
62. Ibid., 110.
63. Quoted in ibid., 112.
64. Ibid., 113.
65. Ibid., 111.
66. Quoted in ibid., 113.
67. Quoted in ibid.
68. Quoted in ibid., 114.
69. Quoted in ibid., 115.
70. Sampson, *Blacks in Blackface,* 387.
71. Daughtry, *Sissieretta Jones,* 117.
72. Charters, *Nobody,* 45.
73. Stearns and Stearns, *Jazz Dance,* 77–78.
74. Quoted in Daughtry, *Sissieretta Jones,* 164.
75. Gross, "The Black Patti," 4.
76. Ibid., 7.
77. Ibid., 4, 6.
78. Charters, *Nobody,* 45.
79. Quoted in Gross, "The Black Patti," 6.
80. Daughtry, *Sissieretta Jones,* 133.
81. Ibid., 175.
82. Ibid., 175–76.
83. Ibid., 175.
84. Stearns and Stearns, *Jazz Dance,* 78.

85. Ibid., 251.

86. Ida Forsyne Oral History Tapes, Hatch-Billops Collection, Inc., New York.

87. Stearns and Stearns, *Jazz Dance,* 251.

88. Ibid., 78.

89. LeRoi Antoine, *Achievement: The Life of Laura Bowman* (New York: Pageant Press, 1961), 219, 221.

90. Sampson, *Blacks in Blackface,* 364.

91. Mapp, *Directory of Blacks in the Performing Arts,* 36.

92. Sampson, *Blacks in Blackface,* 364.

93. Antoine, *The Life of Laura Bowman,* 207.

94. Fletcher, *100 Years of the Negro in Show Business,* 177.

95. Stearns and Stearns, *Jazz Dance,* 252.

96. Fletcher, *100 Years of the Negro in Show Business,* 177.

97. Stearns and Stearns, *Jazz Dance,* 253.

98. Ida Forsyne Oral History Tapes, Hatch-Billops Collection.

99. Hughes and Meltzer, *Black Magic,* 92.

100. Sampson, *Blacks in Blackface,* 159, 313, 318, 366, 446, 467, 483, 491, 585.

101. Ibid., 366.

102. Ida Forsyne Oral History Tapes, Hatch-Billops Collection.

103. Sampson, *Blacks in Blackface,* 366.

104. Brooks Atkinson, *Conjur, New York Times,* 1 November 1938, 27.

105. Hughes and Meltzer, *Black Magic,* 92.

106. Quoted in Stearns and Stearns, *Jazz Dance,* 257.

107. New York *Amsterdam News,* 23 October 1982, 30.

108. Ida Forsyne Oral History Tapes, Hatch-Billops Collections.

109. Stearns and Stearns, *Jazz Dance,* 77.

4. THE EARLY BLACK DRAMATIC ACTRESS

1. Sampson, *Blacks in Blackface,* 354.

2. Southern, *Biographical Dictionary of Afro-American and African Musicians,* 74.

3. "Inez Clough, Actress Dies," *Amsterdam News,* 29 November 1933 (Black Theatre Scrapbook Collection; Schomburg Center for Research in Black Culture, The New York Public Library, Astor, Lenox and Tilden Foundations, hereafter referred to as Schomburg), 6:27.

4. Sampson, *Blacks in Blackface,* 354.

5. Sampson, quoted in *The Ghost Walks,* 370.

6. Sampson, *Blacks in Blackface,* 263, 354.

7. Southern, *Biographical Dictionary of Afro-American and African Musicians,* 75.

8. Sampson, *Blacks in Blackface,* 354.

9. "Lafayette Theatre," *New York Age,* 16 November 1916, 6.

10. *New York Age,* 18 June; 13 July; 17 August; 12 October 1916.

11. "Lafayette Theatre," *New York Age,* 19 October 1916, 6.

12. Louis Sherwin, "The Colored Players at the Garden Theatre," *Globe*, 6 April 1917, *Granny Maumee* Clippings, Lincoln Center.

13. Charles Darnton, "Negro Players Display Talent at the Garden," *World*, 6 April 1917, *Granny Maumee* Clippings, Lincoln Center.

14. Walton, "Negro Actors Make Debut in Drama," *New York Age*, 12 April 1917, 6.

15. Johnson, *Black Manhattan*, 175–78.

16. "Lafayette Theatre," *New York Age*, 7, 21 June; 1 July; 2, 16 August; 20 September; 4, 18 October; 1, 15, 29 November; 29 December 1917; 12 January 1918.

17. Phyllis Klotman, *Frame by Frame* (Bloomington, IN: Indiana University Press, 1979), 533.

18. Sampson, *Blacks in Blackface*, 408–09.

19. "Good Negro Musical Play (*The Chocolate Dandies*) *New York Times*, 2 September 1924, 22.

20. Em Jo Basshe, *Earth* (New York: Macaulay, 1927), vi.

21. Walter Rigdon, ed., *The Biographical Encyclopedia and Who's Who of the American Theatre* (New York: James H. Heinemann, 1966), 15.

22. *Earth*, Clippings, Lincoln Center.

23. Ibid., *Herald-Tribune*.

24. Ibid., 10 March 1927, New York *Graphic*.

25. Atkinson, "The Play (*Sinin' Sister*)," *New York Times*, 10 March 1927, 23.

26. "Inez Clough Scores Remarkable Hit at Playwrights' Theatre," *Amsterdam News*, 16 March 1927, Black Theatre Scrapbook, Schomburg, 3:23.

27. Rigdon, *Who's Who of the American Theatre*, 52.

28. Bide Dudley, "The New Play (*Wanted*)," *Evening World*, 5 July 1928, 18.

29. Rigdon, *Who's Who of the American Theatre*, 21.

30. "When White Is Black (*Harlem*)," *New York Times*, 21 February 1939, 30.

31. Arthur Ruhl, " 'Harlem' Negro Melodrama of Racketeer Sort," *Herald-Tribune*, *Harlem* clippings, Lincoln Center.

32. *New York Times*, 14 September 1929, 17.

33. " 'De Promis' Lan' a Negro Pageant," *New York Times*, 28 May 1930, 31.

34. Randolph Edmonds, "The Little Theatres," *Afro-American*, 21 November 1931, Black Theatre Scrapbook, Schomburg, vol. 4.

35. Rigdon, *Who's Who of the American Theatre*, 43.

36. Robert Garland, *World-Telegraph*, 2 January 1932, 18.

37. Burns Mantle, *Savage Rhythm*, *Daily News*, 1 January 1932, *Savage Rhythm* Clippings, Lincoln Center.

38. "Vivian Baber Is Star of 'Rhythm,' " *Chicago Defender*, 9 January 1932, Black Theatre Scrapbook, Schomburg, vol. 4.

39. Atkinson, " 'Way Down South," *New York Times*, 1 January 1932, 30.

40. Klotman, *Frame by Frame*, 127.

41. "Inez Clough, Actress Dies," *Amsterdam News*, 29 November 1933, Black Theatre Scrapbook, Schomburg, 6:27.

42. Sampson, *Blacks in Blackface,* 115–17, 119.

43. Sampson, *The Ghost Walks,* 191, 392–93, 400.

44. Sampson, *Blacks in Blackface,* 116, 174, 234, 258, 309.

45. Sampson, *The Ghost Walks,* 460–63.

46. Rigdon, *Who's Who of the American Theatre,* 34.

47. Sampson, *Blacks in Blackface,* 263–64.

48. Sampson, quoted in *The Ghost Walks,* 481–82.

49. "Bert Williams in *Lode of Koal,*" *New York Times,* 2 November 1909, 9.

50. Sampson, quoted in *The Ghost Walks,* 487.

51. Ibid., 534.

52. Black Theatre Scrapbook, Schomburg, vol. 2.

53. Sampson, *Blacks in Blackface,* 459.

54. Black Theatre Scrapbook, Schomburg, vol. 2.

55. Sampson, *Blacks in Blackface,* 110, 458.

56. Thompson, *The Lafayette Players, 1915–1932,* 209.

57. Anita Bush Oral History Tape, Hatch-Billops Collection.

58. Black Theatre Scrapbook, Schomburg, 2:5.

59. Walton, "In Quest of Egyptian Princess," *New York Age,* 22 March 1917, 6.

60. Rennold Wolf, "Colored Actors Present 3 Plays," *Telegraph,* 6 April 1917, *Granny Maumee* Clippings, Lincoln Center.

61. "Negro Drama Capably Played," *American,* 6 April 1917, *Granny Maumee* Clippings, Lincoln Center.

62. Unidentified review, *Granny Maumee* Clippings, Lincoln Center.

63. Walton, "Negro Actors Make Debut in Drama," *New York Age,* 12 April 1917, 6.

64. Sampson, *Blacks in Blackface,* 36.

65. Sister Francesca Thompson, "The Lafayette Players, 1917–1932," in *The Theatre of Black Americans,* vol. 2, edited by Errol Hill (Englewood Cliffs, NJ: Prentice-Hall, 1980), 14.

66. Ibid.

67. Thompson, *The Lafayette Players, 1915–1932,* 8.

68. Thompson, "The Lafayette Players, 1917–1932," 14.

69. Sampson, *Blacks in Blackface,* 120.

70. Thompson, "The Lafayette Players, 1917–1932," 14–16.

71. Thompson, *The Lafayette Players, 1915–1932,* 15.

72. Quoted in ibid., 18.

73. Ibid., 22.

74. Thompson, "The Lafayette Players, 1917–1932," 19.

75. Thompson, *The Lafayette Players, 1915–1932,* 28–41.

76. Ibid., 32, 35.

77. Ibid., 43–44.

78. Quoted in ibid., 44.

79. Ibid., 49, 53, 63.

80. Quoted in ibid., 54–55.

81. Quoted in ibid., 63.

82. Thompson, "Final Curtain for Anita Bush," *Black World* (July 1974): 60.

83. Thomas Cripps, *Slow Fade to Black: The Negro in American Film, 1900–1942* (New York: Oxford University Press, 1977), 182.

84. Anita Bush Scrapbook, Hatch-Billops Collection.

85. Klotman, *Frame by Frame*, 84.

86. Anita Bush Scrapbook, Hatch-Billops Collection.

87. Rigdon, *Who's Who of the American Theatre*, 47.

88. "Minstrels over the Adelphi (*Swing It*)," *New York Times*, 23 July 1937, 17.

89. Rosetta LeNoire, taped interview with author, 11 January 1989, New York.

90. Ibid.

91. Anita Bush Scrapbook, Hatch-Billops Collection.

92. *Amsterdam News*, 23 February 1974, B-15.

93. Thompson, *The Lafayette Players, 1915–1932*, 239.

94. Ibid.

95. Dido Johnson, "The Truly Startling Story of Laura Bowman," *Daily Citizen* (no city), 30 December 1933, *Jezebel* Scrapbook, Lincoln Center.

96. Antoine, *The Life of Laura Bowman*, 11, 49, 71, 83–89.

97. Ibid., 114.

98. Ibid., 111–14, 140–42.

99. Ibid., 114.

100. Ibid., 112, 134.

101. Ibid., 140, 154, 161–63.

102. Ibid., 140, 160–64.

103. Ibid., 181, 239.

104. Ibid., 181.

105. Ibid., 183–87, 190–91.

106. Ibid., 194–206.

107. Ibid., 208, 210–11.

108. Ibid., 211.

109. Ibid.

110. Ibid., 212, 219–21.

111. Ibid., 220.

112. Ibid., 223.

113. Rigdon, *Who's Who of the American Theatre*, 45.

114. Antoine, *The Life of Laura Bowman*, 255.

115. Ibid., 227.

116. Ibid., 250, 254.

117. Ibid., 286, 290, 307.

118. Ibid., 317–18.

119. Ibid., 323.

120. "Lafayette Theatre," *New York Age*, 15 June; 6 July; 5 October 1916.

121. White, "Lafayette Theatre," *New York Age*, 15 June 1916, 6.

122. White, "Madame X," *New York Age*, 21 September, 1916, 6.

123. Antoine, *The Life of Laura Bowman*, 320–21.

124. Ibid., 321.

125. White, "Lafayette Theatre," *New York Age*, 2 November 1916, 6.

126. "Lafayette Theatre," *New York Age*, 25 January; 1, 4 February, 12, 26 April; 10, 24 May 1917.

127. Antoine, *The Life of Laura Bowman*, 322.

128. Ibid., 325–29.

129. Ibid., 329.

130. Alain Locke and Montgomery Gregory eds., *Plays of Negro Life* (New York: Harper & Bros., 1927; reprinted, Westport, CT: Negro Universities Press, 1970), 419–20.

131. Fannie E. F. Hicklin, *The American Negro Playwright, 1920–1964* (Ann Arbor, MI: University Microfilms, 1965), 128–29.

132. Mitchell, *Black Drama*, 83.

133. Rigdon, *Who's Who of the American Theatre*, 10.

134. "Ethiopians Act 'Salomé,'" *New York Times*, 8 May 1923, 22.

135. Percy Hammond, "Oscar Wilde's 'Salomé' by the Ethiopian Art Theatre," *Herald-Tribune*, Black Theatre Scrapbook, Schomburg, 2:27.

136. John Corbin, "Jazzed Shakespeare," *New York Times*, 16 May 1923, 22.

137. Antoine, *The Life of Laura Bowman*, 329, 335.

138. Rigdon, *Who's Who of the American Theatre*, 31.

139. "New York Critics Clash in Criticism of 'Meek Mose,'" *Afro-American*, 18 February 1928, Black Theatre Scrapbook, Schomburg, vol. 1.

140. "Mayor at Opening of Negro Theatre (*Meek Mose*)," *New York Times*, 7 February 1928, 30.

141. Ibid.

142. "New York Critics Clash in Criticism of 'Meek Mose,'" *Afro-American*, 18 February 1928, Black Theatre Scrapbook, Schomburg, vol. 1.

143. Quoted in ibid.

144. Quoted in ibid.

145. Antoine, *The Life of Laura Bowman*, 380, 418–19.

146. Thompson, *The Lafayette Players, 1915–1932*, 215–16.

147. Quoted in ibid., 216.

148. Ibid.

149. Quoted in ibid., 217.

150. Quoted in ibid.

151. Ibid., 217–20.

152. Ibid., 220–24.

153. Mitchell, *Black Drama*, 88.

154. *Wade in de Water* Program, Black Theatre Scrapbook, Schomburg, vol. 1.

155. Thompson, *The Lafayette Players, 1915–1932*, 224–25.

156. Ibid., 226–29.

157. Antoine, *The Life of Laura Bowman*, 344, 437.

158. Rigdon, *Who's Who of the American Theatre*, 43.

159. Atkinson, *Sentinels, New York Times*, 26 December 1931, 15.

160. Ibid.

161. Richard Lockridge, "Play of the South (*Sentinels*)," *New York Sun*, 26 December 1931, 10.

162. Mantle, "Colored Players Add Vivid Performances to New Lulu Vollmer Drama," *New York Daily News, Sentinels* Clippings, Lincoln Center.

163. Rigdon, *Who's Who of the American Theatre*, 49.

164. John Mason Brown, " 'The Tree,' New Drama," *Post*, 13 April 1932, *The Tree* Clippings, Lincoln Center.

165. "Calls New Play Morbid Drama," *Amsterdam News*, 20 April 1932, Black Theatre Scrapbook, Schomburg, 4:43.

166. "Lynching Gets Wee Bit Closer to Stage: 'Tis *Tree* This Time," *Chicago Defender*, 23 April 1932, Black Theatre Scrapbook, Schomburg, 4:47.

167. Brown, " 'The Tree,' " *Post*, 13 April 1932, *The Tree* Clippings, Lincoln Center.

168. Atkinson, (*The Tree*), *New York Times*, 13 April 1932, 23.

169. Antoine, *The Life of Laura Bowman*, 227.

170. Thompson, *The Lafayette Players, 1915–1932*, 231–32.

171. Ibid., 233.

172. Klotman, *Frame by Frame*, 152, 521, 624.

173. Antoine, *The Life of Laura Bowman*, 349, 353.

174. Atkinson, "Voodoo Incantation (*Louisiana*)," *New York Times*, 28 February 1933, 15.

175. " 'Louisiana,' New Negro Drama, Opens Here," *Brooklyn Daily Eagle*, Black Theatre Scrapbook, Schomburg, vol. 1.

176. Rigdon, *Who's Who of the American Theatre*, 29.

177. Mantle, "Gods of Vengeance and 'Louisiana,' " *Daily News*, 1 March 1933, Black Theatre Scrapbook, Schomburg, vol. 1.

178. Antoine, *The Life of Laura Bowman*, 360–63, 381.

179. Ibid., 370.

180. Ibid., 365.

181. Ibid., 372–73.

182. Rigdon, *Who's Who of the American Theatre*, 25.

183. Atkinson, *Jezebel, New York Times*, 20 December 1933, 26.

184. Johnson, "The Truly Startling Story of Laura Bowman," Lincoln Center.

185. Bushnell Dimond, " 'Jezebel' Reported Akin to 'Green Hat,' " *Columbus Journal Dispatch*, 31 December 1933, *Jezebel* Scrapbook, Lincoln Center.

186. Atkinson, *New York Times*, 20 December 1933, 26.

187. Garland Mackey, "Former Local Girl Stars in 'Drums of Voodoo,' " *Washington Tribune*, 1 February 1934, Black Theatre Scrapbook, Schomburg, vol. 5.

188. Rigdon, *Who's Who of the American Theatre*, 54.

189. Lockridge, " 'Yesterday's Orchid' Is Acted at the Fulton," *New York Sun*, 6 October 1934, Collection of Newspaper Clippings of Dramatic Criticism of Plays Produced in New York, 1934–35, Lincoln Center.

190. Kauf, *Yesterday's Orchid, Variety*, 9 October 1934, Collection of Newspaper Clippings 1934–35, Lincoln Center.

191. Lockridge, " 'Yesterday's Orchid,' " *New York Sun*, 6 October 1934, Col-

lection of Newspaper Clippings 1934–35, Lincoln Center.

192. Antoine, *The Life of Laura Bowman*, 374–75.

193. Ibid., 375.

194. Sampson, *Blacks in Blackface*, 341.

195. Craig, *Plumes in the Dust*, unidentified Washington, D.C., newspaper, 27 October 1936, *Plumes in the Dust* Clippings, Lincoln Center.

196. Rigdon, *Who's Who of the American Theatre*, 39.

197. Antoine, *The Life of Laura Bowman*, 419–20.

198. Rigdon, *Who's Who of the American Theatre*, 20.

199. Mitchell, *Black Drama*, 102.

200. Antoine, *The Life of Laura Bowman*, 420.

201. *Post*, 1 November 1938, *Conjur* Clippings, Lincoln Center.

202. Atkinson, *Conjur, New York Times*, 1 November 1938, 27.

203. Ibid.

204. Sampson, *Blacks in Blackface*, 341.

205. Rigdon, *Who's Who of the American Theatre*, 39.

206. Robert Sylvester, "Hold Your Hats, Folks, They're Doing Shows as They Did in '28," *Daily News*, 17 March 1939, Collection of Newspaper Clippings 1938–39, Lincoln Center.

207. Atkinson, *Please Mrs. Garibaldi, New York Times*, 17 March 1939, 24.

208. Sylvester, "Hold Your Hats," *Daily News*, 17 March 1939, Collection of Newspaper Clippings 1938–39, Lincoln Center.

209. *Please Mrs. Garibaldi, Variety*, 22 March 1939, Lincoln Center.

210. Antoine, *The Life of Laura Bowman*, 420.

211. Ibid., 421.

212. Ibid.

213. Sampson, *Blacks in Blackface*, 341.

214. Klotman, *Frame by Frame*, 385.

215. Antoine, *The Life of Laura Bowman*, 421.

216. Ibid., 422.

217. Ibid., 421–22.

218. Ibid., 422, 429.

219. Lewis Nichols, *Jeb, New York Times*, 22 February 1946, 20.

220. Mitchell, *Black Drama*, 125.

221. Antoine, *The Life of Laura Bowman*, 429.

222. Waters, *Jeb, Variety*, 13 February 1946, *Jeb* Clippings, Lincoln Center.

223. Rigdon, *Who's Who of the American Theatre*, 24.

224. Nichols, *New York Times*, 22 February 1946, 20.

225. Irene Kittle Kamp, "Goodbye to a Good Play," *Jeb* Clippings, Lincoln Center.

226. Antoine, *The Life of Laura Bowman*, 423.

227. Ibid.

228. Mitchell, *Black Drama*, 122.

229. Rigdon, *Who's Who of the American Theatre*, 4.

230. Antoine, *The Life of Laura Bowman*, 432.

231. Ibid., 429, 432–33.

232. Ibid., 438.

233. Ibid., 439.

234. Ibid., 435.

235. Ibid., 436.

236. Ibid., 436–37.

237. Ibid., 436.

238. Ibid., 435.

239. Ibid., 436.

240. "Laura Bowman Is Dead," *New York Times,* 31 March 1957, 89.

241. Bordman, *The American Musical Theatre,* 159.

242. Southern, *Biographical Dictionary of Afro-American and African Musicians,* 275.

243. Logan and Winston, *Dictionary of American Negro Biography,* 441.

244. Mrs. Marion Douglas Quick, a.k.a. Maranantha Quick, taped interview with author, 29 June 1988, New York.

245. Southern, *Biographical Dictionary of Afro-American and African Musicians,* 275.

246. Logan and Winston, *Dictionary of American Negro Biography,* 441–42.

247. Ibid., 442.

248. Quick, taped interview with author.

249. Ibid.

250. Quoted in Woll, *Dictionary of the Black Theatre,* 157.

251. Logan and Winston, *Dictionary of American Negro Biography,* 442.

252. Southern, *Biographical Dictionary of Afro-American and African Musicians,* 275.

253. Logan and Winston, *Dictionary of American Negro Biography,* 441.

254. Quick, taped interview with author.

255. Quoted in Sampson, *Blacks in Blackface,* 134.

256. Logan and Winston, *Dictionary of American Negro Biography,* 442.

257. Sampson, *Blacks in Blackface,* 277.

258. Sampson, *The Ghost Walks,* 466, 68.

259. Quoted in ibid., 468.

260. Ibid., 479.

261. Quoted in ibid., 511.

262. Ibid., 516.

263. Ibid., 517.

264. Quick, taped interview with author.

265. Sampson, *Blacks in Blackface,* 405.

266. Thompson, *The Lafayette Players, 1915–1932,* 250, 252.

267. Ibid., 46, 50–59.

268. Quoted in Logan and Winston, *Dictionary of American Negro Biography,* 442.

269. Thompson, *The Lafayette Players, 1915–1932,* 59–60.

270. Ibid.

271. Ibid., 60.

272. Quoted in ibid.

273. Ibid., 61–62.

274. Ibid., 64–65.

275. White, "Forty-Five Minutes from Boston," *New York Age,* 2 November 1916, 6.

276. Thompson, *The Lafayette Players, 1915–1932,* 64.

277. Ibid., 40, 46, 64–65.

278. "Lafayette Theatre," *New York Age,* 30 November; 26 December 1916; 29 March; 26 April; 1 July; 2, 16, 30 August; 13 September; 29 November; 29 December 1917.

279. "Lafayette Theatre," *New York Age,* 18 June; 6 July; 5 October 1916; 25 January; 4 February; 10, 24 May; 7, 21 June; 20 September; 4, 18 October; 1, 15 November 1917; 12 January 1918.

280. White, "Lafayette Theatre," *New York Age,* 18 June 1916, 6.

281. "Dramatics and Athletics," *New York Age,* 17 May 1917, 6.

282. Klotman, *Frame by Frame,* 168.

283. Sampson, *Blacks in Blackface,* 36–37.

284. Logan and Winston, *Dictionary of American Negro Biography,* 442.

285. Ibid.

286. Ibid.

287. Quick, taped interview with author.

288. Ibid.

289. Rigdon, *Who's Who of the American Theatre,* 400.

290. Quick, taped interview with author.

291. Sampson, *Blacks in Blackface,* 271.

292. Ibid., 118.

293. Quick, taped interview with author.

294. George Goldsmith, " 'Abraham's Bosom,' at Provincetown, Is Tragedy of South," *Herald-Tribune,* 31 December 1926, Clippings, Lincoln Center.

295. " 'In Abraham's Bosom' a Powerful Tragedy," *New York Times,* 31 December 1926, 10.

296. Ibid.

297. Wilfred J. Riley, "In Abraham's Bosom," *Billboard,* Clippings, Lincoln Center.

298. Goldsmith, " 'Abraham's Bosom,' at Provincetown, Is Tragedy of South," *Herald-Tribune,* 31 December 1926, Clippings, Lincoln Center.

299. F.J.G., "The Village Comfortable 'In Abraham's Bosom,' " *Telegram,* 31 December 1926, Clippings, Lincoln Center.

300. "De Blind Man Stood in de Road and Cried," *Evening Post,* 31 December 1926, *In Abraham's Bosom* Clippings, Lincoln Center.

301. J. A. Rogers, "J. A. Rogers Gives His Impression of New Play at the Provincetown," *Amsterdam News,* 5 January 1927, 11.

302. J. S. "In Abraham's Bosom," *Evening World,* 31 December 1926, Clippings, Lincoln Center.

303. "Play of Negro Spiritual Goes on View in 'Village,' " *American,* 31 December 1926, *In Abraham's Bosom* Clippings, Lincoln Center.

304. *New York Times,* 13 February 1927, *In Abraham's Bosom* Clippings, Lincoln Center.

305. "In Abraham's Bosom," *Billboard,* Clippings, Lincoln Center.

306. Rigdon, *Who's Who of the American Theatre,* 23.

307. Mantle, " 'House of Shadows' Stocked with Stocks," *Daily News,* 27 April 1927, Collection of Newspaper Clippings, 1926–27, Lincoln Center.

308. Stephen Rathbun, "Haunted House," *Sun,* 22 April 1927, Collection of Newspaper Clippings, 1926–27, Lincoln Center.

309. Hammond, " 'The House of Shadows,' a Dull and Hysterical Nightmare at the Longacre," *Herald-Tribune,* 22 April 1927, Collection of Newspaper Clippings, 1926–27, Lincoln Center.

310. *Billboard, In Abraham's Bosom* Clippings, Lincoln Center.

311. Mitchell, *Black Drama,* 85.

312. Rigdon, *Who's Who of the American Theatre,* 13.

313. Atkinson, "Native Opera of the South," *New York Times,* 5 October 1926, *Deep River* Clippings, Lincoln Center.

314. New York *Post,* 9 October 1926, *Deep River* Clippings, Lincoln Center.

315. Riley, "In Abraham's Bosom," *Billboard,* 15 January 1927, Clippings, Lincoln Center.

316. Rigdon, *Who's Who of the American Theatre,* 11.

317. *Theatre Arts* (February 1928): *Coquette* Scrapbook, Lincoln Center.

318. Mantle, " 'Coquette' Great for Helen Hayes," *Coquette* Scrapbook, Lincoln Center.

319. "Massa Harris' Way down South in Dixie," *Evening Post,* 12 November 1927, Collection of Newspaper Clippings, 1927–28, Lincoln Center.

320. Quick, taped interview with author.

321. Ibid.

322. *Coquette* Programs, Lincoln Center.

323. Thompson, *The Lafayette Players, 1915–1932,* 226.

324. Logan and Winston, *Dictionary of American Negro Biography,* 442–43.

325. Quick, taped interview with author.

326. Logan and Winston, *Dictionary of American Negro Biography,* 442.

327. Ibid.

328. Quoted in ibid., 443.

329. Quoted in ibid.

330. Quoted in ibid.

331. Quoted in ibid.

332. Ibid.

333. Ibid.

334. Quick, taped interview with author.

335. Logan and Winston, *Dictionary of American Negro Biography,* 443.

336. Rigdon, *Who's Who of the American Theatre,* 47.

337. Atkinson, "Drama of the Race Riot 'Stevedore,' Put On by the Theatre Union," *New York Times,* 19 April 1934, Clippings, Lincoln Center.

338. Ibid.

339. Ibid.

340. *World-Telegram,* 2 October 1934, Collection of Newspaper Clippings, 1934–35, Lincoln Center.

341. " 'Stevedore' Begins a Return Engagement in 14th Street," *Evening Post,* 2 October 1934, Clippings, Lincoln Center.

342. *Stevedore* Clippings, Lincoln Center.

343. *Playbill,* 1 October 1934, 8.

344. Rigdon, *Who's Who of the American Theatre,* 47.

345. *Stevedore* Programs, 10 December 1934; 24 December 1934.

346. Lloyd Lewis, "Rough and Thrilling," *Daily News,* 27 December 1934, *Stevedore* Clippings, Lincoln Center.

347. Mitchell, *Black Drama,* 98.

348. Rigdon, *Who's Who of the American Theatre,* 39.

349. Gilman Lawrence, "George Gershwin's New Opera, 'Porgy and Bess,' Produced by the Theatre Guild," *Herald-Tribune,* 11 October 1935, Collection of Newspaper Clippings, 1935–36, Lincoln Center.

350. "Porgy and Bess," *Variety,* 16 October 1935, Collection of Newspaper Clippings, 1935–36, Lincoln Center.

351. Leonard Liebling, "Gershwin Music Stirs Hearers at 'Porgy and Bess,'" *American,* 11 October 1935, Collection of Newspaper Clippings, 1935–36, Lincoln Center.

352. Mantle, "'Porgy and Bess,' Stirs Audience," *Daily News,* 11 October 1935, Collection of Newspaper Clippings, 1935–36, Lincoln Center.

353. Mitchell, *Black Drama,* 98.

354. *Porgy and Bess* Programs, Lincoln Center.

355. Rigdon, *Who's Who of the American Theatre,* 28.

356. Richard Watts, Jr., "The Little Foxes," *Herald-Tribune,* 16 February 1939, Collection of Newspaper Clippings, 1938–39, Lincoln Center.

357. Ibid.

358. George Ross, "Decay of the South Hellman Play Theme," *World-Telegram,* 16 February 1939, Collection of Newspaper Clippings, 1938–39, Lincoln Center.

359. Atkinson, "The Little Foxes," *New York Times,* 16 February 1939, Collection of Newspaper Clippings, 1938–39, Lincoln Center.

360. Ibee, "The Little Foxes," *Variety,* 22 February 1939, Collection of Newspaper Clippings, 1938–39, Lincoln Center.

361. John Cambridge, "'The Little Foxes' a Story of Southern Aristocrats," *Daily Worker,* 17 February 1939, Collection of Newspaper Clippings, 1938–39, Lincoln Center.

362. Pollock, "Lillian Hellman's 'The Little Foxes' Opens at the National Theater with Tallulah Bankhead and Excellent Cast," *Brooklyn Daily Eagle,* 16 February 1939, Collection of Newspaper Clippings, 1938–39, Lincoln Center.

363. Quick, taped interview with author.

364. Ibid.

365. Mantle, *Best Plays of 1939–40,* 476.

366. Etta Moten, "'Black Patti's' Early Triumph," *Chicago Journal and Guide,* 8 June 1940, Moorland-Spingarn Research Center, Howard University, Washington, D.C.

367. Quick, taped interview with author.

368. Ibid.

369. LeNoire, taped interview with author.

370. Rigdon, *Who's Who of the American Theatre,* 36.

371. Nichols, "On Whitman Avenue," *New York Times*, 9 May 1946, 28.

372. Press Release, *On Whitman Avenue* Scrapbook, Lincoln Center.

373. Nichols, "On Whitman Avenue," *New York Times*, 9 May 1946, 28.

374. Morehouse, *Sun*, 9 May 1946, *On Whitman Avenue* Scrapbook, Lincoln Center.

375. Barnes, *Tribune*, 9 May 1946, *On Whitman Avenue* Scrapbook, Lincoln Center.

376. Garland, *Journal*, 9 May 1946, *On Whitman Avenue* Scrapbook, Lincoln Center.

377. Rice, *Post*, 9 May 1946, *On Whitman Avenue* Scrapbook, Lincoln Center.

378. William Hawkins, *Telegram*, 9 May 1946, *On Whitman Avenue* Scrapbook, Lincoln Center.

379. *Variety*, 22 May 1946, *On Whitman Avenue* Scrapbook, Lincoln Center.

380. Rice, " 'On Whitman Avenue,' Boldly Faces the Negro Problem," *New York Post*, 9 May 1946, Clippings, Lincoln Center.

381. Ibee, "On Whitman Avenue," *Variety*, 15 May 1946, Clippings, Lincoln Center.

382. Garland, " 'Whitman Avenue' Presented at Cort," *Journal American*, 9 May 1946, Clippings, Lincoln Center.

383. George Freedley, " 'On Whitman Avenue.' Well-Intentioned but Slight Drama of Race Relations," *New York Morning Telegraph*, 10 May 1946, Collection of Newspaper Clippings, 1945–46, Lincoln Center.

384. Logan and Winston, *Dictionary of American Negro Biography*, 443.

385. Quick, taped interview with author.

386. Ibid.

387. "Abbie Mitchell Goes to Perpetual 'Summertime,' " *Amsterdam News*, 26 March 1960, 4.

388. Dick Campbell, taped interview with author, 7 May 1990, New York.

389. Logan and Winston, *Dictionary of American Negro Biography*, 443.

390. "Abbie Mitchell Goes to Perpetual 'Summertime,' " *Amsterdam News*, 26 March 1960, 4.

391. Logan and Winston, *Dictionary of American Negro Biography*, 443.

5. EPILOGUE

1. Mitchell, *Black Drama*, 144.

SELECTED BIBLIOGRAPHY

A number of key articles are not included here. They are, however, cited in the notes. As a guide to further research, the following list provides the most important sources on the subject.

Antoine, LeRoi. *Achievement: The Life of Laura Bowman.* New York: Pageant Press, 1961.

Armstead-Johnson, Helen. *Black America on Stage.* New York: CASTA, The Graduate School and University Center of CUNY, 1978.

Charters, Ann. *Nobody: The Story of Bert Williams.* New York: Macmillan, 1970.

Cuney-Hare, Maude. *Negro Musicians and Their Music.* Washington, D.C.: Associated Publishers, 1936.

Daughtry, Willa E. *Sissieretta Jones: A Study of the Negro's Contribution to Nineteenth-Century American Concert and Theatrical Life.* Ann Arbor, MI: University Microfilms, 1968.

Cripps, Thomas, *Slow Fade to Black: The Negro in American Film, 1900–1942.* New York: Oxford University Press, 1977.

Emery, Lynne Fauley. *Black Dance in the United States from 1619 to 1970.* New York: Dance Horizons, 1980.

Fletcher, Tom. *100 Years of the Negro in Show Business.* New York: Burdge, 1954.

Greenfield, Elizabeth T. *A Brief Memoir of the "Black Swan."* London: n.p., 1853.

Haskins, James. *Black Theater in America.* New York: Thomas Y. Crowell, 1982.

Hill, Errol. *The Theater of Black Americans.* 2 vols. Englewood Cliffs, NJ: Prentice-Hall, 1980.

————. *Shakespeare in Sable: A History of Black Shakespearean Actors.* Amherst, MA: University of Massachusetts Press, 1984.

Huggins, Nathan. *Harlem Renaissance.* New York: Oxford University Press, 1971.

Hughes, Langston, and Milton Meltzer. *Black Magic: A Pictorial History of the Negro in American Entertainment.* Englewood Cliffs, NJ: Prentice-Hall, 1968.

Isaacs, Edith. *The Negro in the American Theatre.* New York: Theatre Arts, 1947. Reprint. College Park, MD: McGrath, 1968.

Johnson, James Weldon. *Black Manhattan.* New York: Alfred A. Knopf, 1940. Reprint. New York: Arno Press and the *New York Times,* 1968.

Klotman, Phyllis, *Frame by Frame.* Bloomington, IN: Indiana University Press, 1979.

Mapp, Edward. *Directory of Blacks in the Performing Arts.* Metuchen, NJ: Scarecrow Press, 1978.

Mitchell, Loften. *Black Drama: The Story of the American Negro in the Theatre.* New York: Hawthorn Books, 1967.

Sampson, Henry T. *Blacks in Blackface: A Source Book on Early Black Musical Shows.* Metuchen, NJ: Scarecrow Press, 1980.

————. *The Ghost Walks: A Chronological History of Blacks in Show Business, 1865–1910.* Metuchen, NJ: Scarecrow Press, 1988.

Southern, Eileen. *Biographical Dictionary of Afro-American and African Musicians.* Westport, CT: Greenwood Press, 1982.

Stearns, Marshall, and Jean Stearns. *Jazz Dance: The Story of American Vernacular Dance.* 2d ed. New York: Macmillan, 1970.

Thompson, Sister Francesca. *The Lafayette Players, 1915–1932: America's First Dramatic Stock Company.* Ann Arbor, MI: University Microfilms, 1972.

Toll, Robert C. *Blacking Up: The Minstrel Show in Nineteenth-Century America.* New York: Oxford University Press, 1974.

Woll, Allen. *Directory of the Black Theatre: Broadway, Off-Broadway, and Selected Harlem Theatre.* Westport, CT: Greenwood Press, 1983.

————. *Black Musical Theatre: From "Coontown" to "Dreamgirls."* Baton Rouge, LA: Louisiana State University Press, 1989.

INDEX